PAPER TO DIGITAL

PAPER TO DIGITAL

Documents in the Information Age

ZIMING LIU

LIBRARIES
UNLIMITED
A Member of the Greenwood Publishing Group
Westport, Connecticut • London

Library of Congress Cataloging-in-Publication Data

Liu, Ziming, 1965–
   Paper to digital : documents in the information age / Ziming Liu.
      p.   cm.
   Includes bibliographical references and index.
   ISBN 978–1–59158–620–3 (alk. paper)
   1. Information resources—Use studies.   2. Electronic information resources—Use studies.
3. Information resources—Evaluation.   4. Electronic information resources—Evaluation.
5. Documentation.   6. Communication in learning and scholarship.   7. Electronic publishing.
8. Digital preservation.   9. Information behavior.   10. Libraries and the Internet.   I. Title.
   ZA3060L58   2008
   020—dc22   2008021120

British Library Cataloguing in Publication Data is available.

Library of Congress Catalog Card Number: 2008021120
ISBN: 978–1–59158–620–3

First published in 2008

Libraries Unlimited, 88 Post Road West, Westport, CT 06881
A Member of the Greenwood Publishing Group, Inc.
www.lu.com

Printed in the United States of America

The paper used in this book complies with the
Permanent Paper Standard issued by the National
Information Standards Organization (Z39.48–1984).

10 9 8 7 6 5 4 3 2 1

CONTENTS

ILLUSTRATIONS

TABLES

FIGURES

FOREWORD

As with Gutenberg's invention of printing with moveable type, the development of digital technology has had a profound impact on the creation and use of documents and records of every kind. New technology ordinarily inspires enthusiastic speculation, in this case about cyberspace and "the virtual." Further, the exciting potential of digital computing has induced sustained efforts to model human cognitive behavior in digital terms, invoking imagined mental "states of knowledge" and "knowledge structures."

Enthusiastic exploration of the future impact of the cybersphere and "the virtual" has an important place. But, as with earlier technical innovations, many predicted changes have not occurred and many actual changes were unexpected. Further, when technology is deployed, the result is a socio-technical system. A dynamic interaction is to be expected, but the outcome is a product of human behavior as well as the technology—and human nature and the design of human beings have remained unchanged.

All these factors increase the need for thoughtful analysis carefully grounded in day-to-day realities. What is refreshing about Ziming Liu's book is that he explores the world of documents and of reading intelligently but calmly. He looks intelligently at what is and seeks to ascertain underlying relationships.

This book provides a useful synthesis. The prior works of others have been systematically surveyed and summarized. A series of exploratory surveys probe basic relationships. A plausible picture emerges of the distinctive features of digital documents, the uncertainty of preservation, changes in scholarly publishing, and the likely future role of paper. Preferences between reading online and on paper are situational and cultural and gender differences can be detected. Professor Liu, formerly a librarian, discusses the implications of these changes for libraries and other information services.

What Professor Liu has found should not really surprise us. The move to electronic documents has greatly increased the use of paper because, for many purposes, humans tend to prefer reading texts on paper to reading on glowing screens. That digital technology has made it easier to create, revise, and distribute documents really means that there are more documents for us to read and, since we often prefer to read paper, more printing results.

The several surveys that Professor Liu reports are exploratory and not intended to be definitive. They provide pointers. They indicate what is likely to be prevalent and they suggest relationships. His findings are best seen as well-informed hypotheses and a basis for future research. This is as it should be. Understanding progresses by a sequence of speculation, prospecting, testing, refutation, and new speculation.

We should be grateful for this timely overview. Not only is it a convenient summary, but, also, it can form the basis for him as well as others to strengthen and extend our understanding of documents and their role in society.

Michael Buckland
Berkeley, CA

ACKNOWLEDGMENTS

This book would not have been possible without the considerable support and encouragement of a number of individuals.

I am indebted to Michael Buckland for writing the Foreword and for his many constructive suggestions for this book. I also deeply thank him for his guidance and for introducing me to the theoretical and historical perspectives of the document when I was a doctoral student at the University of California at Berkeley.

I greatly appreciate my colleagues at RICOH California Research Center, especially Peter Hart and David Stork, for offering me opportunities to explore trends in documents and their implications, and for stimulating my thinking of documents in the office environment.

I would like to thank all my colleagues at San Jose State University, especially Ken Haycock and Linda Main, for the institutional support. I also acknowledge students at San Jose State University, to whom I owe more intellectual benefits and stimulations than I can readily describe. I am grateful to those who participated in the surveys and gave me invaluable insights. Research assistance by Leslie Elmore and David Gross is also greatly appreciated.

Special thanks must go to Blanche Woolls, the consulting editor of Libraries Unlimited, for providing valuable comments. Her support when she was director of the School of Library and Information Science at San Jose State University earns my deep gratitude. I also thank Manish Sharma, project manager at Aptara Inc., for his efficient job in the production process.

1

INTRODUCTION

Since the time of the Sumerians, documents and their supporting technologies have continued to evolve at an unprecedented rate. Wilbur Schramm (1988) documents that it took at least 50 million years for society to progress from spoken language to writing, about 5,000 years from writing to printing, about 500 years from printing to the development of sight–sound media (photography, the telephone, sound recording, radio, television), yet fewer than fifty years from the first of the sight–sound media to the modern computer.

In recent years, computing and networking technologies have caused an unprecedented change in the creation, storage, distribution, and access of documents. Many technologies appear to expand the document boundaries and extend the traditional definition of documents. As documents are being used in new ways, it has become increasingly important to examine their changing characteristics and their resultant impacts on individuals, organizations, and society.

As Gorman (2003) notes: "We need to absorb the new ways of doing things that digital technology makes possible, but we must do so in such a way that technology serves the values and purposes of librarianship. Technology is not the answer to everything. Thinking that we live in some kind of epochal period for communication leads people to think that libraries have either to be abolished or so completely transformed as to be unrecognizable—both unlikely hypotheses." New technology permits new service opportunities, generates new expectations, shapes new behaviors, and also raises new challenges. Yet, in the rush from a paper-based environment to the digital world, it seems important to deliberate on a fundamental question: what are the effects and implications of this transition? This is a very broad question that needs to be answered as we embark on the digital era; but to approach such a grand question, many more specific research questions must be addressed.

QUESTIONS FOR THE TWENTY-FIRST CENTURY INFORMATION PROFESSIONAL

- The development of information technologies has had a profound impact on scholarly publishing as well as on the way in which scholars communicate with each other. How have collaboration and the volume of information production been changed? Will researchers use older documents under today's Internet environment where new information is easily available? What are the implications for library and information services?

- The new characteristics of digital documents (e.g., fluidity and intangibility) pose unprecedented challenges for the preservation of digital information. What are the potential conflicts between the new reality of digital information and the traditional expectations in the print environment? Many people have low confidence and trust in digital preservation. Are there any possible ways to regain people's trust in digital preservation?

- Technological advances have made e-books and digital libraries a reality. Although reading on glowing screens remains an option undesirable to many, digital technologies have already begun to affect reading practice and behavior as people spend more time reading online. How has people's reading behavior been changed in the online reading environment? How do people handle electronic documents (e.g., annotation and printing out) when they read?

- To what extent do male and female readers differ in the preference for reading media and in the overall satisfaction with online reading? Does gender play a role in handling digital documents and in the changes of reading behavior?

- The advent of the Internet as a new and widely used channel for the delivery of information raises the question of the credibility of information. In the Internet environment, everybody has a potential to become a publisher. No one has to review the content of these documents before they are posted on the Web. Because of its ephemeral nature and the lack of a traditional refereed process, selecting credible information from the sheer amount of information has become a challenging task for most users, especially young people. What criteria do people use in evaluating the credibility of scholarly information on the Web? How do the criteria differ from evaluating the quality of information on print media? What are the impacts of document features (e.g., authorship, institutional affiliation, URL domains, and number of references) on credibility perceptions? How do young people identify "experts" and come to trust the veracity of what they read on the Web? When young people assess the credibility of scholarly information on the Web, what features make the information *credible*? And what features make the information *less credible*? What are the implications for library and information professionals (e.g., user education)?

- Credibility perception is deeply embedded in and heavily influenced by its social and cultural contexts. Cultural differences may have a significant impact on credibility assessment. What are the similarities and differences in credibility assessment between students in different cultures?

- The prevalence of electronic resources is affecting the way students and scholars use print resources and physical libraries. How do they make choices between print and electronic resources? How do circumstances affect the selection of use between traditional and digital libraries? How are print and electronic resources best served?

- Paper has been the most popular document medium for nearly twenty centuries. What will be the future of paper in the digital age?

As one might expect, the answers to these questions are very complex. There is no single right answer. It is hoped that the remainder of this book will strengthen the reader's understanding of these emerging issues.

This book is an attempt to provide some answers as a result of years of studying these changing characteristics and their resultant implications. My hope is that it may contribute in some small way, if it could encourage further research in this area.

OVERVIEW OF THE BOOK

The major task of this book is to explore the changing characteristics of documents and resultant implications through an examination of emerging issues. Examples include trends in transforming scholarly communications; trust in the preservation of digital information; changes in reading behavior in the digital environment; perceptions of the credibility of scholarly information on the Web; user preferences for and use of print and electronic resources; and the future of paper in the digital age. This book is based on extensive statistics and six separate surveys. In the process of approaching these research questions, we have made use of whatever methods seem most appropriate to help us find answers.

This book is organized into ten chapters. At first glance, these chapters may seem scattered. But if considered under the larger framework of document life cycles, the relationship becomes apparent: creation (Chapter 3 on publishing), storage (Chapter 4 on digital preservation), and utilization (Chapters 5–6 on reading behavior and Chapters 7–8 on credibility assessment). Without taking related aspects into account, our understanding of the changing characteristics of documents and their resultant impacts will be incomplete.

Chapter 1 offers a brief summary of the changing characteristics of documents and lists a number of research questions that deserve our scrutiny.

Chapter 2 provides a sorted overview of the evolution of documents and its impacts from the following aspects: information density, longevity, uniqueness, duplicability, mobility, connectivity, and integration. It focuses on the consequences of the shift from print to digital media. By looking back on their evolution, we are able to see how the notions and functions of documents change over time, and the resulting impacts on individuals, organizations, and society.

The development of information technologies has had a profound impact on scholarly publishing as well as on the way in which scholars communicate with each other. Traditional scholarly publishing is experiencing tremendous pressure for change under the confluence of the following forces and trends: the exponential growth of information production, the dramatic increase in subscription fees, the increasing storage cost of printed documents, and the increasing power and availability of digital technology. Chapter 3 concentrates on trends in transforming scholarly publishing and their implications. It examines how collaboration and the volume of information production have changed over the past century, from 1900 to 2000. As scholarly publishing and libraries are shifting from paper-based formats to electronic formats, new information is becoming easily accessible. However, an analysis of citation data reveals that we should not forget that in the Internet age where new information is easily obtained, people are still using older documents. The availability of information in a variety of formats and channels requires an examination of how print and electronic resources are best served, and to understand how users make choices between library-provided materials and information available on the Web. One important role of librarians is to educate the public about the value of library resources and to "help users select the best resources and overcome information overload" (Tenopir, 2003).

One of the grand challenges raised by the transition from print to digital documents is "how we are to preserve the historic record in an electronic era where change and speed is valued more highly than conversation and longevity" (Kuny, 1997). There is a recent wave of literature addressing issues of the preservation of digital media. The discussion of digital preservation is often overshadowed by the fragility of digital media, technological obsolescence, and standards. Little attention has been given to the most critical barrier in the preservation of digital information: the potential conflicts between the new reality of digital information and the expectation of people. Based on our survey of 110 people who have intensive experience in handling digital information, such as office workers, students, teachers, scientists, and administrators, we find that the major challenge in the digital preservation is to increase people's confidence and trust in digital information. Trust is critical when there is a lack of confidence. In the preservation context, there is a need for trust because of the uncertainty about digital preservation. In Chapter 4, we apply a concept derived from our analysis of monetary currency, called "institutional guarantee," to the development of trusted systems for the preservation of digital information. We believe that the creation of an institutional guarantee for trusted digital preservation is instrumental to increasing people's confidence and trust in digital media, since there are no precedents for preserving documents of this nature.

The advent of digital media and the growing collection of digital documents have a profound impact on reading. It was argued that the development of digital libraries "is participating in a general societal trend toward shallower, more fragmented, and less concentrated reading" (Levy, 1997). Previous studies attempt to explore reading in the digital environment through examining the evolution of reading or observing how people read documents (especially electronic documents) within a specific period of time. Instead of observing how people read electronic documents, Chapter 5 attempts to investigate reading behavior in the digital environment by analyzing how people's reading behavior has changed over the past ten years. We show that with an increasing amount of time spent on reading electronic documents, a screen-based reading behavior is emerging. This screen-based reading behavior is characterized by spending more time on browsing and scanning, keyword spotting, one-time reading, nonlinear reading, and reading more selectively, while less time is spent on in-depth reading, concentrated reading, and decreasing sustained attention. Annotating and highlighting while reading is a common activity in the print environment. However, this "traditional" pattern has not yet migrated to the digital environment when people read electronic documents. In an increasingly digital environment, readers (especially younger readers) are likely to gradually develop the screen-based reading behavior, and to increasingly use a variety of strategies (e.g., browsing and key-word spotting) to cope with the information-abundant environment. On the other hand, readers will continue to use print media for much of their reading activities, especially in-depth reading. In-depth reading usually involves annotating and highlighting. People's preference for paper as a medium of reading (especially in-depth reading) also implies that paper is unlikely to disappear in the digital age.

Rather than deprecating digital technology as hurting our reading quality in the online environment, we should embrace its potential and expect technological advances will reduce the problems even further. While many people don't see digital libraries as a place for "concentrated reading" but as a gateway to access information, we should keep in mind that technology is constantly improving and reading practices themselves are evolving.

Gender differences in Web information seeking have attracted considerable interest. However, little is known about gender differences in online reading behavior. Chapter 6 takes a closer look at gender differences in the online reading environment. We find that female readers have a stronger preference for paper as a reading medium than male readers, whereas male readers exhibit a greater degree of satisfaction with online reading than females. Additionally, males and females differ significantly on the dimension of selective reading and sustained attention. Factors affecting gender differences in the online reading environment are discussed. The circumstances affecting the choice of reading media are also presented.

Scholarly examination of credibility is perhaps among the oldest lines in communication research, originating with the ancient Greeks (Self, 1996). The arrival of the Internet raises this old concept to a new level of importance. The Internet provides people easier access to a huge amount of information more than at any previous time in human history. With the Web, it matters little where the Web site is. However, the improved access to documents makes which document to believe and use a much more central concern (Buckland and Plaunt, 1997). Tenopir (2003) notes: "It is unclear how the move from paper-based library collections to digital collections is affecting scholarly work.... Librarians face new challenges in reaching students who only access library resources online and have grown up with the Web. It is difficult to make sure that such students know how to select appropriate resources, evaluate the quality of what they select, and use these resources well regardless of format or medium." There is an increasing awareness among library and information professionals of the need to educate users on how to evaluate the Internet information. Understanding how people assess the credibility of scholarly information on the Web would enable us to improve user education, and eventually better inform and empower users. Based on a survey of 128 students in the United States, Chapter 7 focuses on identifying factors and circumstances influencing students' perceptions of the credibility of scholarly information on the web. In addition to the four types of source credibility proposed by previous studies (presumed, reputed, surface, and experienced credibility), Chapter 7 shows that two other types of source credibility (verifiable and cost-effort credibility) play a significant role in shaping students' perceptions of credibility.

Cultural differences may have a strong impact on credibility assessment. There is a pressing need to understand how people from different cultures use scholarly information from the Web to do assignments and conduct research. In Chapter 8, we investigate how Chinese students make credibility assessments of Web-based information for their research, and what evaluation criteria they employ. Our findings indicate that presumed, reputed, and surface credibility have a stronger impact on undergraduate students than on graduate students in credibility assessment. Graduate students tend to value experienced credibility more than undergraduate students. Undergraduate students predominantly rely on author's name/reputation/affiliation as well as the Web site reputation for their credibility evaluation. In contrast, graduate students focus more than undergraduate students on information accuracy/quality. We also discuss similarities and differences in credibility assessment between American and Chinese students.

The proliferation of Web-based information not only raises the need for credibility studies, but also affects the use of library-provided electronic resources as well as print resources. Marcum (2003) points out that "the greatest research needs are to understand how roles and responsibilities change in the digital environment.... User studies become increasingly important as libraries move from housing materials to providing electronic access to them, becoming gateways to materials instead of owners. To succeed in this new business, libraries must understand how users look for and find the information they need." Chapter 9 explores the extent to which graduate students in a metropolitan university setting use print and electronic resources. Circumstances that affect the selection of use between digital and traditional libraries are also discussed. Our findings indicate that users desire a hybrid information environment in which online information does not supplant information in print but adds new access opportunities for users to choose. Digital and traditional libraries have their unique advantages and limitations; they satisfy the information needs of users in different circumstances. Each plays a different role and serves the needs of users in varied ways. Digital libraries offer a wide range of new access opportunities that are absent in the traditional environment, including remote access, 24-hour access, and multiple users for single sources. However, the desire for physical browsing, the need for immediate help from a "real" person, and the desire for communal space for learning— make a case for the importance of the traditional service environment. The hybrid library is likely to be a model for the foreseeable future.

In Chapter 10, we pull together many of the findings in previous chapters and discuss the future of paper in the digital age. Despite different extents in preferences among different genders and cultures (e.g., American, Chinese, and Mexican), we find that the preference for reading printed text remains strong. This clearly indicates that paper is unlikely to disappear in the digital age, because reading print media is deeply embedded in tradition. Digital as well as print media have their unique advantages and limitations. Each plays a different role and serves the needs of users in different circumstances. Even though people are likely to read more from a screen than from a printed page in the future, we must also keep in mind that readers' purposes and preferences are very diverse, and that there is not a single format that is ideal to all. It is unlikely that digital media will render traditional books and libraries obsolete in the foreseeable future. In the digital age, printing for serious reading and annotating remains one of the major driving forces for the increasing consumption of paper.

REFERENCES

Buckland, M. and Plaunt, C. (1997). Selecting Libraries, Selecting Documents, Selecting Data. Retrieved November 29, 2007, from http://people.ischool. berkeley.edu/~buckland/isdl97/isdl97.html.

Gorman, M. (2003). For Libraries, Digitization Is a Factor, Not the Future. *Logos*, 14(2), 66–68.

Kuny, T. (1997). The Digital Dark Ages? Challenges in the Preservation of Electronic Information. *63rd IFLA Council and General Conference*. Retrieved October 29, 2007, from http://www.ifla.org/IV/ifla63/63kuny1.pdf.

Levy, D.M. (1997). I Read the News Today, Oh Boy: Reading and Attention in Digital Libraries. In *Proceedings of the 2nd ACM International Conference on Digital Libraries* (pp. 202–211). New York, NY: ACM Press.

Marcum, D.B. (2003). Research Questions for the Digital Era Library. *Library Trends*, 51(4), 636–651.

Schramm, W. (1988). *The Story of Human Communication: Cave Painting to Microchip.* New York, NY: McGraw-Hill.

Self, C.C. (1996). Credibility. In: M.B. Salven and D.W. Stacks (Eds.), *An Integrated Approach to Communication Theory and Research* (pp. 421–441). Mahwah, NJ: Lawrence Erlbaum Associates, Publisher.

Tenopir, C. (2003). Electronic Publishing: Research Issues for Academic Librarians and Users. *Library Trends*, 51(4), 614–635.

2

THE EVOLUTION OF DOCUMENTS AND ITS IMPACTS

Our perception and understanding of documents is usually shaped by the documents we conventionally use. Traditionally, documents were denoted as "textual and text-like records" (e.g., books or a pile of printed records). This was the prevailing view of documents before the arrival of digital documents. The traditional notion of documents no longer accommodates emerging forms of digital documents. The concept of what constitutes a document is becoming increasingly complicated and amorphous (Buckland, 1997; Schamber, 1996). With the resurgence of interest about various fundamental issues of documents, more careful attention to the historical examination of the evolution of various aspects of documents is warranted. It is not the purpose of this chapter to review various definitions of a document; rather it attempts to provide a sorted overview of the evolution of documents. This approach would enhance our understanding of how the notions and functions of documents change over time, and the resulting impacts on individuals, organizations, and society.

INFORMATION DENSITY

The earliest known evidence of writing originated approximately 6000 years ago. Sumerians began inscribing symbols on clay tablets to record business transactions. Since then, the storage capacity of documents began its long

---

This chapter is based on: Liu, Z. (2004). The Evolution of Documents and Its Impacts. *Journal of Documentation*, 60(3), 279–288.

journey of evolution. As measured by the number of characters per square inch, the information density of the document is expanding exponentially with the development of its supporting technologies. According to Conway (1996), the information density is 34 characters per square inch on clay tablets, 141 on illuminated manuscripts, 10,000 on microfilms, 106,200 on floppy disks, and 50 million on optical disks. He finds that there is a relative stability in information density before the arrival of the printing press, and electronic technologies offer the opportunity for expanding storage capacity.

The growth in information density of documents has a number of profound impacts.

The growth in information density suggests documents are increasingly becoming more invisible to the human eye and more dependent on reading devices. Cook (1994) observes that "for the first time in 3,500 years of archival activity we produce records that do not exist to the human eye—unlike Babylonian clay tablets, Egyptian papyrus, Roman and medieval parchment, modern paper, even microfilm." Unlike information recorded on a paper-based medium, information on digital media is invisible to the human eye. The higher information density of digital media also implies a paradigm shift in the preservation practice: from preservation to access. Preserving digital information without making it accessible is simply a waste of effort.

Information storage media have evolved toward greater information density, keeping the information operationally remote from the reader. Paper is a medium that allows direct exchange of information with its readers. Readers of paper-based media can access information without any type of device or intermediary as long as they are literate.

Deeply embedded in the context of "seeing is believing" of the printed culture for so many generations, people's confidence and trust in digital information is negatively associated with intangibility. How to regain people's confidence and trust becomes one of the grand challenges in digital preservation (see Chapter 4 for more discussion).

The dependence on reading devices for accessing information invisible to the human eye inevitably creates a barrier for those who do not have a reading device or who do not know how to use it. If everything becomes digital, those people are essentially denied the opportunity to access information. Many studies investigate the social, cultural, and economic factors leading to the digital divide. However, examining the evolution of information capacity shows that the dependence on reading devices is also a contributing factor leading to the digital divide.

LONGEVITY

Document media and their associated production methods have always evolved together. For example, sticks evolved together with cuneiform on clay tablets, knives with runes on wood tablets, styluses with marks on wax tablets, brushes with ink on vellum, typewriters with ribbon-ink on rag stock, and color laser printers with toner on paper. Both medium and tool define document attributes such as duplicability, fixity, and information density (Jean, 1992). It should be noted here that all documents require a base for receiving the information and a way of recording that information. The survival of information tends to depend on the properties of both. For example, information incised on stone may last for millennia, but information painted on stone (unless carefully protected) will disappear much more rapidly.

In the process of evolution of document media, the physical life of document media, with a handful of exceptions (microfilm and WORM), is becoming increasingly shorter over time. The growing information capacity of documents also gives rise to one central dilemma of recording history. As Conway (1996) further notes: "Our capacity to record information has increased exponentially over time while the longevity of the media used to store the information has decreased equivalently." For example, the classical Greek script in the stone is still legible after twenty-two centuries; words in Shakespeare's first printed edition of sonnets are legible after nearly four centuries; many microfilms carried by pigeons during the siege of Paris in 1870 are still readable today. Digital media, however, can become unreadable within a decade (Rothenberg, 1995).

Because of the fragility of digital media and the rapid obsolescence of reading devices, we cannot guarantee that digital information can be readable after a decade, let alone 500 years. Traditionally, people tend to think of preservation periods in terms of centuries instead of a few years. The short physical life and fragility of digital documents implies that we need constant backup in order to protect sudden loss of information. Being digital means fragile and ephemeral. Marcum (2003) notes that "the preservation of traditional materials must therefore continue even in the digital era, or one might say *especially* in the digital era because no medium is more susceptible to media decay and loss through obsolescence than the tapes and disks containing magnetic bytes and bits."

UNIQUENESS

With the improvements of document technologies, the distinction between the original and the copy is gradually blurring. Before the printing press, documents were reproduced by hand copying. It was almost impossible that documents looked exactly the same. The distinction between an original and a copy was very clear, even if the original and the copy were hand copied by the same person. In Europe and North America, a technique known as "letter press" was used to copy documents handwritten with ink. It was not difficult to identify an original and a copy (Rhodes and Streeter, 1999). The development of typewriters at the end of the nineteenth century made it possible to reproduce a document that looked like the original. For a lengthy document, however, the difference between the original and the copy was still easy to distinguish. In the case of carbon paper, the copy approximated the original, but it was easy enough to tell them apart. The improvements in photocopying technology made it possible to produce copies that looked exactly the same as the original. Over the years, it has become very difficult to distinguish the original and the copy (O'Toole, 1994). Nowadays it is almost impossible to identify the differences between an original and a copy in digital media. O'Toole (1994) notes: "The traditional understanding of physically unique records is difficult to sustain in a world of intangible, constantly changing, interconnected bits of data."

The trend in the decreasing uniqueness of documents has a number of interesting implications. For example, is the traditional distinction in archiving practice between an original and a copy still relevant? Should we purposefully make it possible to distinguish an original from a copy?

Traditionally, information organizations deal directly with "information-as-thing." For example, libraries deal with books, museums display objects, and archives handle records. The "differences in their physical attributes affect how the stored items can be handled" (Buckland, 1991). Rayward (1998) observes that with the proliferation of "information-as-thing" being represented electronically, "the physical distinctions between the different formats or media of record disappear." He further notes that digitization "eliminates physical distinctions between types of records and thus, presumably, the need for institutional distinctions in the management of the systems with which these records are handled."

The networked environment together with the digital format of objects opens a new level of interlinking the collections of archives, libraries, museums, and the like; hence a new level of opportunities to access and study such objects. But—at least in some instances—it might be a fundamental difference whether we handle the unique, watermarked and signed original or an undistinguishable volatile copy. And the systems have to respect these differences.

DUPLICABILITY

Documents have also evolved toward ease in duplication. Consider the duplication of a clay tablet, the duplication of a paper document with carbon paper or using a photocopier, duplication of a microfilm, or duplication of digital media. It took a copyist in the ninth and tenth centuries a day to copy four pages, roughly 2 bits per second (Jean, 1992). It takes years to duplicate 1 gigabit of information on clay tablets, days or weeks with the copier, hours or days on microfilm, but only seconds or minutes on digital media.

Document technologies evolved not only toward ease in duplication, but also toward reduction in setup cost. The invention of the Gutenberg press led to the start of the first information revolution as the printed word was used to disseminate ideas and concepts throughout the world. One of the most significant characteristics of the Gutenberg press and the subsequent technologies is high setup costs with low marginal costs for subsequent copies. Over the last 500 years, print technologies continued to depend on this key economic characteristic. Similarly, the invention of the Remington typewriter revolutionized the use of paper in industry, since it enabled low-volume replication at relatively moderate marginal per-copy costs. Strassmann (1985) offers an excellent insight on the changing production cost pattern. He states: "Advances in machine tools make it possible to disseminate widely the technical means for publishing. Unit costs of printed matter decline rapidly as the length of a production run increases. Gradual innovation reduces the initially high setup cost of the Gutenberg process so that the marginal cost of an additional print approaches the average cost. This is why the xerography process can be classified as the perfection of Gutenbergian concepts and its final evolutionary stage rather than as belonging to some other developmental phase." Print on demand can be viewed as a continuation or extension of the Gutenberg process.

The ease in duplication and low cost for production has a number of interesting impacts.

The development of printing for mass production of documents is a milestone in the development of documents. With the invention of movable type and the printing press, the laborious hand copying of texts became obsolete. Documents could be produced at low cost, and therefore could reach the general public. The improvement of technologies for mass production was an impetus for a more democratic society with an informed populace. The great increase in the circulation of knowledge stimulated the creation of additional knowledge. The development of the steam driven rotary press, along with the spread of the railroads and the innovation in producing cheap paper, also resulted in profound changes in the nature and breadth of written literacy, from the elites to the masses. The proliferation of copiers and fax machines further speeds the pace of human discourse (Eisenstein, 1983; Levien, 1991).

Reproduction and distribution of documents at lower cost has historically made it more difficult for any one or a small entity to control all access (Compaine, 1988). Low setup cost also enables everybody to reproduce and distribute information (e.g., posting information on the Web, and distributing information via e-mail lists). Everyone (who has a computer and Internet access) has the potential to become a publisher. The ease of duplicating and distributing information raises the issue of trust or credibility of information. While information is more readily available than ever before, selecting credible information from a vast amount of information becomes a daunting task. This problem is becoming even more severe under the World Wide Web (WWW), since there is an increasing number of documents coming from self-publishing. No one has to review the content of these documents before they are posted on the Web. Information on the Web is ephemeral and can be altered easily. Gorman (2003) raises a concern of the "highly likely destruction of the environment of authenticity that has allowed scholarship and learning to flourish." For more discussion on credibility, see Chapters 7 and 8.

Unlike their predecessors, digital documents are easy to duplicate. This provides unsurpassed opportunities to back up for preservation purposes. However, the development of digital technologies and the popular use of digital documents also pose an unprecedented challenge to protect copyright. Samuelson (1991; 1995) states hand copying was very time consuming and reproduced only a very limited number of copies. Even though rapid mass production was possible, printing presses required considerable expense to operate. Using photocopy machines is time consuming and difficult to make "perfect" copies. Copyright protection will become more and more difficult with the ease in the reproduction and distribution of digital documents.

In the digital realm, duplicability also has serious impacts on the reliability and authenticity of digital documents. Gorman (2003) warns that we may return to the Manuscript Age when hand-copied documents were so routinely altered, making it difficult to find the original message. In an article published in the *New Yorker* on November 5, 2007, Grafton presents a very interesting example: "In a scriptorium lit by the sun, a scribe could mistakenly transcribe a 'u' as an 'n,' or vice versa. Curiously, the computer makes the same mistake. If you enter *qualitas*—an important term in medieval philosophy—into Google Book Search, you'll find almost two thousand appearances. But if you enter 'qnalitas' you'll be rewarded with more than five hundred references that you wouldn't necessarily have found. Sometimes the scanner operators miss pages, or scan them out of order. Sometimes the copy is not in good condition. The cataloguing data that identify an item are often incomplete or confusing. And the key terms that Google provides in order to characterize individual books are sometimes unintentionally comic."

Duplicability makes it easy for the "stolen" document to be passed off as someone else's work. And even worse, the deliberate malignant changes introduced by a third person may skew the author's opinions, findings, and beliefs expressed in a document and thus do harm to the author's reputation. In order to prevent such misbehavior, we have to find new ways to "fix" digital information (e.g., digital watermark).

MOBILITY AND FLUIDITY

Document medium defines the portability of the document. Stone and clay tablets are extremely localized media, usually constrained to local use. Bamboo, papyrus, and wood are very localized media, but with the aid of transportation, they can be used by people at a greater distance. Paper and microfilm are less localized media, and they can by accessed more easily. Electronic documents are not localized. With telecommunication connections, an electronic document can be used from anywhere and by multiple people simultaneously. For the first time in human history, it is possible to disseminate written messages to a group of scattered audiences without reproducing the messages in multiple copies and distributing the copies across geographical space (Neavill, 1984).

The introduction of printing promotes a uniformity of documents that has been previously unavailable. However, the arrival of digital documents introduces individuality, enabling customization of documents. Kircz (1998) argues that the digital environment, where storage and presentation are no longer integrated, enables one to shatter the linear structure of the article and therefore serves the needs of readers more responsively. On the other hand, Brown and Duguid (2000) warn that a sense of community arises from reading the same text, and a personalized environment may make it hard to find common ground.

Bruno Latour (1986) describes documents as "immutable mobiles" where immutability denotes the unchangibility of documents while mobility means the ability to circulate. These two qualities tend to pull against one another. Brown and Duguid (2000) note that "paper and ink established a useful balance—light enough to be portable, but fixed enough to be immutable. Printing maintained that balance.... Yet with the digital, while transportation and mobility are enhanced, immutability is diminished. Some documents, such as Web pages, are constantly changing." Identification is therefore problematic in the digital environment. For example, how we can tell that a Web document we see this month is the same one when we see it next month. The same uniform resource locator (URL) does not necessarily guarantee the same content. The average life of a link on the Web is about forty-five days. It is difficult to predict whether the link will be there next week or even tomorrow (John, 2000).

However, we should not ignore that fluidity has its impassable charm. It is difficult to imagine a world without computers or word processors, when revising a 250-page book means completely retyping all corrected pages, or when changing a few words or lines in one page means time-consuming effort in figuring out if they are in the same page. Fluidity and ease in updating are ideal for certain type of documents (especially telephone directories and airline schedules). However, other types of documents (e.g., legal documents and certificates) are not subject to change because of their inherent nature of fixity. To a certain extent legal documents today still require handwriting, in that a personal signature is the only appropriate means of authenticating contracts, wills, and sales documents. For example, a letter making a job offer may be sent through fax or e-mail in order to achieve greater speed of reaching the recipient; meanwhile, the letter needs to come by traditional mail to comply with legal requirements and normal practice.

Brown and Duguid (2000) stress, "For all the advantages of fluidity, we should not forget the fixity still has its charms.... In many situations, fixity is more important than fluidity." Fixity is instrumental to maintaining communicative stability and repeatability (Levy, 2001). Fixity is also critical to documents whose major function is evidentiary. Few of us would want to have our Ph.D. certificates be sent by e-mail as Microsoft (MS) Word documents or in portable document format (pdf) files.

To cope with the fluidity in the digital environment, we have to find ways to "fix" digital information (Lynch, 1994). Fixed shots of the developing human knowledge give historical evidence of gradual progress. In the digital environment, the often-changing documents create unprecedented challenges for preservation procedures. Deciding "what is to be collected and preserved" is not a new question. Now, the changing nature of documents creates new problems as to "what to preserve" and more importantly "how often to check."

CONNECTIVITY

Documents are not totally independent. Every document is related to other documents. The publication of a book will generate a body of related documents: revised versions, book reviews, translations, citations, and information in indexes and abstracts. A letter can also trigger one or more responses. Connectivity of documents is further strengthened in the networked environment where related documents are linked together. Theodor Nelson first coined the word "hypertext" in the 1960s. He refers to it as "nonsequential writing—text that branches and allows choices to the reader, best read at an interactive screen. As popularly conceived, this is a series of text chunks connected by links which offer the reader different pathways" (Landow, 1994).

The connectivity of documents has a number of interesting implications.

Traditionally, the boundary of a document is relatively easy to define. However, links between electronic documents make it difficult to define the boundary of a document. For a very long time, the document has been viewed as a static information resource with limited ability for change. In the networked environment, documents are subject to constant change due to the linkage. The proliferation of hyperlinks, by making the unity and boundaries of documents less clear, also affects preservation.

The proliferation of hyperlinks has a number of positive impacts (e.g., immediacy of information accessing), but it also introduces unintended consequences (e.g., fragmented reading). In the print environment, it takes time to locate a related document such as a reference. However, in the networked environment, the connectivity of digital documents enables immediate access of linked documents. It is more convenient for an average user to click a link and access a document than to get a copy of a printed document. With hyperlinks, one can easily maneuver through a document by a simple click from a comfortable chair at midnight—no drive to the library, no finding the call number, no check out and return of items, and no photocopying needed.

The proliferation of hyperlinks has a profound impact on people's reading behaviors such as nonlinear reading. According to a study by Almind and Ingwersen (1997), a document on the Web has an average of nine links. The more links, the greater the potential differences in reading paths. Even for readers who start reading from the same page, what they read may be different depending on which link is activated. Hyper-reading may also reduce the sustained attention to any textual source and lead to more fragmented reading, since each page on the Web has to compete with many other pages for the user's attention. In terms of hypertext linking, the author's conception of the connection's relevance may not be the same as the reader's. Links imposed may not be logically associated with the original topic, which may send readers to a site for no discernible purpose and result in disorientation (Miall and Dobson, 2001; Dobrin, 1994). Birkerts (1994) observes that the younger generation growing up in the digital environment is lacking the ability to read deeply and to sustain a prolonged engagement in reading. In an article, "From Thinkers to Clickers," Thirunarayanan (2003) warns: "As interactions with the Web increase, the clicking and wandering behavior gets more deeply entrenched among human beings. Such aimless cyber wandering eventually becomes a substitute for meaningful thinking." Please see Chapters 5 and 6 for detailed discussions on reading behavior in the digital environment.

INTEGRATION

Paul Otlet, a European documentalist in the early part of the last century, foresaw that radio, television, x-rays, cinema, and microscopic photography would eventually be integrated in a single workstation-like machine, a kind of "mechanical, collective brain" (see Rayward, 1994). There is a trend of integration throughout the evolution of document technologies:

- Because of the difficulty of writing with a quill on parchment or with a stylus on wax, writing was considered a special skill that was not automatically coupled with the ability to read. In twelfth-century England, the most common way of committing words to writing was by dictating to a scribe. Paper technology blurred the boundaries between composing and dictating (Jean, 1992).

- In the domain of paper technology, the typewriter was the key technology for creation, and the file cabinet for storage, mail systems for distribution, and photocopiers for reproduction. Unlike mechanical antecedents, the computer is not restricted to a single role in production or distribution. In fact, technology tends to erase distinctions between the separate processes of creation, reproduction, and distribution (Nunberg, 1993).

- In the earlier ages, different forms of information (e.g., data, image, text, and voice) were separate due to the immaturity of technology and the absence of open standards. Data processing systems handled data, word processing systems handled text, telephone systems handled voice, and photocopiers and microfilm systems handled image. As information contained in these systems becomes digitized, and as standards grow, the opportunity to integrate them unfolds (Tapscott and Caston, 1993).

• The convergence of computing and telecommunications is inevitable as the computer becomes more powerful and communications become more capable of handling rich data. Telecommunications, office equipment, media, publishing, and computing were separate industries through the 1990s. But as the computer becomes an information appliance, the boundaries of distinct industries would blur.

The convergence in information and communication technologies has profound impacts on the society. Largely due to the convergence, it has become impractical to distinguish among video, voice, and data services in the digital environment. Given their very different histories, policies appropriate for one particular technology will not be appropriate for another. A study by Rand concludes that "policies developed separately for telephony, computer communications, broadcasting, and publishing that create artificial distinctions in the emerging information infrastructure should be reviewed, and a consistent framework should be developed that spans all the industries in the unified communications/messaging industry" (Anderson et al., 1995).

CONCLUSION

Paul Otlet foresaw in the early part of last century that a new form of the book should be "(1) less heavy and smaller; (2) uniform in size; (3) on a permanent material; (4) moderate in price; (5) easy to preserve; (6) easy to consult; and (7) continuously produced: that is, copies or duplicates can be produced on request" (Rayward, 1990). While we are moving closer to Otlet's requirements, we are also moving away from his predictions. Looking back on the evolution of documents from various dimensions, we find that many impacts of the transition to digital society are positive (e.g., remote access and rapid distribution of information), and some are negative (e.g., information reliability and tension between reading and attention). Some impacts are intended, while others are unintended or unavoidable (e.g., digital divide, information overload, and copyright protection). It has become increasingly important to examine the changing characteristics of documents and their resultant impacts on individuals, organizations, and society such as

• What are the roles and responsibilities of libraries in an information abundant environment?

• What are the potential conflicts between the new reality of digital information and the traditional expectations in the print environment?

- How has people's reading behavior been changed in the online reading environment?

- What criteria do people use in evaluating the credibility of scholarly information on the Web? How do the criteria differ from evaluating the quality of information on print media?

- How are print and electronic resources best served? How do people favor and select one format over the other?

- What will the future of paper be in the digital age?

REFERENCES

Almind, T.C. and Ingwersen, P. (1997). Informatric Analyses on the World Wide Web: Methodological Approaches to "Webometrics." *Journal of Documentation*, 53(4), 404–426.

Anderson, R.H., Kedzie, C., Bikson, T.K., Keltner, B.R., Ann Law, S., Panis, C., Mitchell, B.M., Pliskin, J., and Srinagesh, P. (1995). *Universal Access to E-mail: Feasibility and Societal Implications.* Santa Monica, CA: Rand.

Birkerts, S. (1994). *The Gutenberg Elegies: The Fate of Reading in An Electronic Age.* Boston, MA: Faber and Faber.

Brown, J.S. and Duguid, P. (2000). *The Social Life of Information.* Boston, MA: Harvard Business School Press.

Buckland, M.K. (1991). Information As Thing. *Journal of the American Society for Information Science*, 42(5), 351–360.

Buckland, M.K. (1997). What Is a "Document?" *Journal of the American Society for Information Science*, 48(9), 804–809.

Compaine, B.M. (Ed.). (1988). *Issues in New Information Technology.* Norwood, NJ: Albex Press.

Conway, P. (1996). *Preservation in the Digital World.* Washington, DC: The Commission on Preservation and Access.

Cook, T. (1994). It's 10 O'clock: Do You Know Where Your Data Are? Retrieved February 22, 2008, from http://web.mit.edu/erm/tcook.tr1995.html.

Dobrin, N.J. (1994). Hype and Hypertext. In C.L. Selfe and S. Hilligoss (Eds.), *Literacy and Computers: The Complications of Teaching and Learning with Technology* (pp. 305–315). New York, NY: Modern Language Association.

Eisenstein, E.L. (1983). *The Printing Revolution in Early Modern Europe.* London, England: Cambridge University Press.

Gorman, M. (2003). *The Enduring Library: Technology, Tradition, and the Quest for Balance.* Chicago, IL: American Library Association.

Grafton, A. (2007, November 5). Future Reading: Digitization and Its Discontents. *New Yorker*, 83(34). Retrieved November 20, 2007, from http://www.newyorker.com/reporting/2007/11/05/071105fa_fact_grafton.

Jean, G. (1992). *Writing: The Story of Alphabets and Scripts.* New York, NY: H.N. Abrams.

John, N.R. (2000). The Ethics of the Click: Users and Digital Information in the Internet Age. *Libri*, 50(2), 129–135.

Kircz, J.G. (1998). Modularity: The Next Form of Scientific Information Presentation? *Journal of Documentation*, 54(2), 210–235.

Landow, G.P. (1994). *Hypertext Theory.* Baltimore, MD: Johns Hopkins University Press.

Latour, B. (1986). Visualization and Cognition: Thinking with Eyes and Hands. *Knowledge & Society,* 6, 1–40.

Levien, R.E. (1991). The Civilising Currency: Documents and Their Revolutionary Technologies. In D. Leebaert (Ed.), *Technology 2001: The Future of Computing and Communications* (pp. 205–239). Cambridge, MA: MIT Press.

Levy, D.M. (2001). *Scrolling Forward: Making Sense of Documents in the Digital Age.* New York, NY: Arcade Publishing.

Lynch, C.A. (1994). The Integrity of Digital Information: Mechanics and Definitional Issues. *Journal of the American Society for Information Science,* 45(10), 737–744.

Marcum, D.B. (2003). Research Questions for the Digital Era Library. *Library Trends,* 51(4), 636–651.

Miall, D.S. and Dobson, T. (2001). Reading Hypertext and the Experience of Literature. *Journal of Digital Information,* 2 (1). Retrieved November 2, 2004, from http://jodi.ecs.soton.ac.uk/Articles/v02/i01/Miall/.

Neavill, G.B. (1984). Electronic Publishing, Libraries, and the Survival of Information. *Library Resources & Technical Services,* 28(1), 76–89.

Nunberg, G. (1993). The Places of Books in the Age of Electronic Reproduction. In R.H. Bloch and C. Hesse (Eds.), *Future Libraries* (pp. 13–37). Berkeley, CA: University of California Press.

O'Toole, J.M. (1994). On the Idea of Uniqueness. *American Archivist,* 57(4), 633–658.

Rayward, W.B. (Ed. and Trans.). (1990). *International Organization and Communication of Knowledge: Selected Essays of Paul Otlet.* Amsterdam, The Netherlands: Elsevier.

Rayward, W.B. (1994). Some Schemes for Restructuring and Mobilising Information in Documents: A Historical Perspective. *Information Processing and Management,* 32(2), 163–175.

Rayward, W.B. (1998). Electronic Information and the Functional Integration of Libraries, Museums and Archives. In E. Higgs (Ed.), *History and Electronic Artefacts* (pp. 207–226). Oxford, England: Clarendon Press.

Rhodes, B.J. and Streeter, W.W. (1999). *Before Photocopying: The Art & History of Mechanical Copying, 1780–1938.* New Castle, DE: Oak Knoll Press.

Rothenberg, J. (1995). Ensuring the Longevity of Digital Documents. *Scientific American,* 272(1), 42–47.

Samuelson, P. (1991). Digital Media and the Law. *Communications of the ACM,* 34(10), 23–38.

Samuelson, P. (1995). Copyright and Digital Libraries. *Communications of the ACM,* 38(4), 15–21 and 110.

Schamber, L. (1996). What Is a Document? Rethinking the Concept in Uneasy Times. *Journal of the American Society for Information Science,* 47(9), 669–671.

Strassmann, P.A. (1985). *Information Payoff.* New York, NY: The Free Press.

Tapscott, D. and Caston, A. (1993). *Paradigm Shift: The New Promise of Information Technology.* New York, NY: McGraw-Hill.

Thirunarayanan, M. (2003). From Thinkers to Clickers: The World Wide Web and the Transformation of the Essence of Being Human. *Ubiquity*, 4 (12). Retrieved November 15, 2007, from http://www.acm.org/ubiquity/views/m_thirunarayanan_8.html.

3

———•◦•———

TRENDS IN TRANSFORMING
SCHOLARLY COMMUNICATIONS

The development of information technology has a profound impact on scholarly publishing as well as on the way in which scholars communicate with each other. Traditional scholarly publishing is experiencing tremendous pressure for change. In recent years, there is a wave of literature focusing on the economy (e.g., cost and pricing) and psychology (e.g., user attitudes and behaviors) of scholarly publishing. Little attention has been given to how the scholarly publishing itself has evolved. Our understanding of electronic publishing and the transition to the paperless society would be incomplete without evidence on trends in transforming scholarly communication.

This chapter focuses on trends in transforming scholarly publishing and their implications. It examines how collaboration and the volume of information production have changed over the past century, from 1900 to 2000. It also explores how older documents are used in today's network environment where new information is easily accessible. Examining these trends would help us understand the impact of the transition from a paper-based environment to a digital environment.

Since the primary concern of this chapter is to examine the trends in scholarly journals over the past century, only journals, which have a long history of publication, are qualified for this longitudinal analysis. We select the following three scholarly journals in three different fields for analysis: *American Journal of Mathematics*, *American Journal of Sociology*, and *Journal of the American*

This chapter is an updated and expanded version of an earlier article: Liu, Z. (2003). Trends in Transforming Scholarly Communications and Their Implications. *Information Processing and Management*, 39(6), 889–898.

Chemical Society. In order to examine the trends in collaboration and volume of information production, we analyze bibliographic data from the following years: 1900, 1910, 1920, 1930, 1940, 1950, 1960, 1970, 1980, 1990, and 2000. Only articles were subject to analysis. Book reviews, letters to the editor, and professional news were not taken into consideration.

TRENDS IN COLLABORATION

Modern research has become increasingly collaborative in nature. In *Little Science, Big Science*, Price (1965) predicts that single-author articles would be extinct by 1980s. Increasing multiple-authorship of research articles has been observed across a wide range of scientific disciplines.

Broad (1981) finds that in the 2800 journals indexed by the Institute for Scientific Information between 1960 and 1980, the mean number of authors per paper increased from 1.67 to 2.58. According to Cronin (2001), the average number of authors per article in the *Science Citation Index* rose from 1.83 in 1955 to 3.9 in 1999.

In an analysis of the *Physical Review* and *Physical Review Letters* over a forty-year period (1951–1991), Sampson (1995) finds that the average number of authors per article grew from 1.7 in 1951 to 2.1 in 1958, and to 3.8 in 1991. On the other hand, the proportion of single-author articles was declining, from 45.1% in 1951 to 36.5% in 1958, and to 14.7% in 1991. Sampson (1995) notes that the rise in the complexity of science to which some attribute this growth in coauthorship, was reflected in the increasing complexity of this simple task over the forty-year period from 1951 to 1991.

In an attempt to study the patterns of authorship in *Poultry Science* from 1981 to 1990, Cason (1992) finds that the percentage of single-author articles in *Poultry Science* shrank from 18.1% in 1960 to 15.1% in 1970, and to 9.8% in 1990. Further, Cason (1992) points out that one consequence of author inflation is that researchers today typically have longer publication lists than those at the same career stage thirty years ago. Koehler and others (2000) find that the average number of authors per article published in the *Journal of the American Society for Information Science* (formerly *American Documentation*) increased from 1.2 to 1.8 over the five decades (1950–1990).

The growth of authorship is perhaps most pronounced in the field of medicine. In an analysis of authorship in the *British Medical Journal*, Drenth (2001) finds that the average number of authors per article increased from 3.92 in 1985 to 4.46 in 1995. From 1975 to 1989, mean authors per article in the *New England Journal of Medicine* increased from 3.9 to 6.4 at a rate of 0.17 authors per article per year (Sobal and Ferentz, 1990). An extreme example is an article in the *New England Journal of Medicine* in 1993, listing 972 authors—an average of one author for every two words in that article! Epstein (1993) explains that the need for a large team of technically

Table 3.1
Average Number of Authors per Article (1900–2000)

Year	Chemistry	Mathematics	Sociology
1900	1.36	1.04	1.00
1910	1.52	1.00	1.02
1920	1.67	1.00	1.00
1930	1.86	1.02	1.07
1940	2.15	1.21	1.07
1950	2.35	1.24	1.13
1960	2.38	1.14	1.66
1970	2.57	1.19	1.35
1980	3.09	1.22	1.49
1990	3.53	1.39	1.53
2000	4.30	1.45	1.58

specialized laboratory workers, the need to accrue scarce resources for research, and the inherent labor intensiveness of projects contributed to the growth in authorship.

Changing patterns in authorship of research articles has been observed across a wide range of scientific disciplines. Reasons behind this phenomenon include, among other things, interdisciplinary research with multiple specialists, pressure to publish, the grant system, and the development of communication technologies (Bordons and Gomez, 2000; see Cronin, 2001 for a brief history of authorship). By looking at the trend of collaborative work, we are in a better position to understand scholarly communication in the digital era and to find the communication media that will aid collaboration the most. In this section, we examine the trend in collaboration by examining authorship in the following three different disciplines: chemistry, mathematics, and sociology, over a 100-year period (1900–2000)

As indicated by Table 3.1, the growth in the average number of authors per article is most noticeable in chemistry, from 1.36 authors per article in 1900 to 2.35 in 1950, and to 4.30 in 2000. The number of authors per article is also growing in mathematics, a discipline widely regarded as being isolated in research. The number of authors per article is steadily increasing, from 1.04 in 1900 to 1.24 in 1950, and to 1.45 in 2000. The race of the growth of authorship is slightly faster in sociology than in mathematics, from all single authorship in 1900 to 1.13 in 1950, and to 1.58 in 2000.

Price (1965) predicts that the single-author articles would be extinct by the 1980s. Single authorship in chemistry is diminishing steadily as the years progress. For example, among 1,298 articles published in the *Journal of the American Chemical Society* in 2000, there are only nineteen single-author articles, accounting for 1.5% of all articles published that year. Over 98.5%

articles have multiple authorships. Thirty-one articles have the authorship of ten authors or more, reflecting 2.4% of all articles published in 2000. This trend is consistent with that in medicine. Constantian (1999) finds that 98% of the articles published in the *New England Journal of Medicine* 100 years ago were sole authored; this figure was less than 5% in the 1990s.

Price's prediction of the disappearance of single authorship is more accurate in certain disciplines such as chemistry and medicine. However, single-author articles are still prevailing in many other fields (e.g., mathematics and sociology). Among forty-nine articles published in the *American Journal of Mathematics* in 2000, twenty-eight articles are single-author articles (57%), twenty two-author articles (41%), and only one three-author article (2%). Among the forty articles published in the *American Journal of Sociology* in 2000, there are twenty-two articles written by single author (55%), thirteen articles by two authors (32.5%), and five articles by three authors (12.5%). Single authorship is still very common in mathematics and sociology. One major factor contributing to this common single authorship is that, unlike chemistry and medicine, mathematics and sociology are not lab or experimental-based disciplines.

The growth in authorship is clearly an indication of the trend in increasing collaboration. In today's organizations, as a result of flatter hierarchies, broader participation, and increasing resource sharing, there is a growing tendency to rely on teamwork. This trend is further supported by networked communications and open-system environments, enabling people who are geographically distributed to work together. The involvement of more people in creating a document implies that the document is essentially a combination of many "information-bricks." Understanding the trend in collaboration would help us design efficient groupware to facilitate collaboration in the teamwork-intensive environment (e.g., in the field of chemistry and medicine).

According to McDonald (1995), data produced by the Institute for Scientific Information show that there was only one paper with 100 or more authors in 1981; this figure rose to 182 in 1994. Papers with more than 200 authors rose from one in 1988 to 98 in 1994. One paper published in the *Physical Review Letters* (1995) devotes the first two of its six pages to the names of all 437 authors and their 35 institutions. Cronin (2001) raises concerns about the "hyperauthorship" phenomenon in scholarly publications. He notes that "coauthorship in itself is not inherently problematic, some of the hidden social practices which it has occasioned." He further points out that "in biomedicine, authorship has irrevocably shed some of its craft associations: to be an author is not necessarily to be a writer. But it should not surprise us. Contemporary science is quite different from 17th-century science in terms of both its social and economic structures. In many areas, interdependence is an inescapable fact of research life, and the idea of the lone scholar something of an anachronism."

VOLUME OF INFORMATION PRODUCTION

Scientific and technical journals are now over 300 years old. It was estimated that by 1800 there were 90 scientific journals worldwide, and this number increased to over 10,000 by 1900. Price (1965) plots the growth of the number of journals since their inception. He points out that the number of journals doubled about every fifteen years. As indicated by the following tables, not only the number of journals, but also the size of journals (e.g., the number of issues and number of articles per journal per year) is expanding. For example, the number of issues of *Journal of the American Chemical Society* has increased from 12 (monthly) in 1900 to 24 (biweekly) in 1960, and to 51 (weekly) in 2000 (see Table 3.2). The number of articles has increased from 107 in 1900 to 1,298 in 2000! The number of pages per year has risen from 414 in 1900 to 5,891 in 1950, and to 13,040 in 2000. The sizes of *American Journal of Mathematics* (see Table 3.3) and *American Journal of Sociology* (Table 3.4) are also increasing, even though they are not as significant as in chemistry.

The explosive growth of scholarly production has a number of profound implications.

Attention to Information

The information explosion has received special attention over the past thirty years. Wurman (1989) notes that a weekday edition of the *New York Times* contains more information than an average person was likely to come across

Table 3.2
Volume of Information Production: *Journal of the American Chemical Society* **(1900–2000)**

Year	Number of issues	Number of articles	Number of pages
1900	12	107	414
1910	12	186	872
1920	12	294	1,358
1930	12	804	2,690
1940	12	907	3,574
1950	12	1,415	5,891
1960	24	1,392	6,500
1970	26	1,056	7,733
1980	27	1,014	8,118
1990	26	1,417	9,846
2000	51	1,298	13,040

Note: Numbers of pages in 1900, 1910, 1920, and 1930 are adjusted to reflect changes in page sizes.

Table 3.3
Volume of Information Production: *American Journal of Mathematics* (1900–2000)

Year	Number of issues	Number of articles	Number of pages
1900	4	26	388
1910	4	24	401
1920	4	18	286
1930	4	58	922
1940	4	67	912
1950	4	66	867
1960	4	49	943
1970	4	54	1,230
1980	4	45	1,206
1990	6	41	1,082
2000	6	49	1,308

in a lifetime in seventeenth-century England. One important implication of the growth in information is the change in reading behaviors. According to Darnton (1989), a reading revolution took place at the end of the eighteenth century. From the Middle Ages until sometime after 1750, people were reading "intensively." They had only a few books to read and they read them over and over again. By 1800 people tended to read things "extensively." They read all kinds of material, especially periodicals and newspapers, and read things only once before racing on to the next item. From the evolution of reading, it is not difficult to imagine that "browsing" or "scanning" is becoming a principal reading pattern in today's information-intensive environment. Please see Chapters 5 and 6 for an in-depth analysis and discussion.

Table 3.4
Volume of Information Production: *American Journal of Sociology* (1900–2000)

Year	Number of issues	Number of articles	Number of pages
1900	6	42	864
1910	6	50	864
1920	6	29	806
1930	6	71	1,080
1940	6	44	938
1950	6	48	622
1960	6	59	662
1970	6	46	1,222
1980	6	70	1,592
1990	6	49	1,640
2000	6	40	1,840

As we embark on the information society, the problem of information overload and the resultant disorientation are increasing. Sandberg-Diment (1987) assures that "more information should presumably present more opportunities for broader vision and understanding. Yet the sheer volume of the data amassed makes almost inevitable the reduction of our focus to what is in the end a very narrow endeavor." The swelling number of documents and the limited amount of time available for each one raises the problem of what Richard Lanham (1997) calls the "economy of attention." In the information-abundant environment, attention has become a scarce resource. How to allocate our attention to information that is most valuable is becoming a vital issue that we are facing today (Levy, 1997). As the quantity of information grows, the ability to derive meaning from a vast body of literature begins to deteriorate. And, as Wurman (1989) points out, "Meaning requires time-consuming thought, and the pace of modern life works against affording us the time to think."

Reading a Smaller Percentage of Journal Articles

While the volume of scholarly production increases dramatically, scholars are constrained by a 168-hour week. This means that it is becoming more and more difficult for scholars to keep pace with the growing scholarly production. As a matter of fact, the average amount of time spent on reading scholarly articles has been relatively constant over the years (Tenopir and King, 1998). This implies that a smaller percentage of scholarly articles will be read. Tenopir and King (1998) find that "in approximately 53% of the journals a scientist reads, he or she reads five or fewer articles a year."

Declining Personal Subscription

The volume of many scholarly journals is getting bigger. This may stimulate people to photocopy articles from heavy bound journal volumes to avoid carrying the complete volume. Another alternative is to subscribe to an electronic version of journals, and print out needed articles for in-depth reading and annotations.

It is more cost-effective for information to be produced electronically. Ironically, the production of new media in addition to print versions incurs new cost for the publishers who will in turn transfer this new cost to customers by increasing subscription fees. Meanwhile, an increased volume of journals also creates pressure to increase subscription fees that in turn discourages people to subscribe.

The increasing subscription fees, together with the trend in reading a fewer percentage of journal articles, tend to prevent individual scholars from purchasing scholarly journals. Professors may not be likely to subscribe to a journal that costs them $5,000 for which they need only a handful of articles.

In such a circumstance, scholars may rely on libraries more for their information needs. This argument is further supported by Tenopir and King's (1998) study. They find that there was a decline in personal subscription to scholarly journals and a steady increase in library-provided articles. They explain that "the cost per reading of articles in infrequently read journals becomes prohibitive," when the subscription prices go up. Scientists tend to shift to use library-provided articles as an alternative to personal journal subscriptions. In a recent study, Tenopir and King (2004) find that there is a steady decline in personal subscriptions since the 1970s. The average number of journal subscriptions by scientists and social scientists was down to just under two subscriptions per person.

Pressure On Libraries

The sheer volume of scholarly literature is a strong driving force for electronic publishing. Odlyzko (1995) points out that in 1870 there were about 840 articles published in mathematics. Today, the number reaches about 50,000 papers published annually. He discusses how the growth in size by scholarly publishing was creating a crisis in the traditional approach to dissemination of research findings. Since the library costs in purchasing and housing the increasing expansion of collections is already very high, there is bound to be a great pressure to change the traditional publishing systems as well as traditional libraries. Buckland (1992) notes that the need of an additional 12 miles of bookshelves to house the increasing collection at the University of California system presents an interesting challenge.

The increasing volume of information production alone would be challenging for libraries to accommodate, but at the same time prices have soared. The price of library subscriptions to periodicals in law, medicine, and physics and chemistry rose by 205%, 479%, and 515% respectively, from 1984 to 2001 (Albee and Dingley, 2001). According to the Association of Research Libraries, serial unit costs rose by 226% from 1986 to 2000. Albanese (2001) observes an alarming scene in libraries: "Serials cancellation exercises have become routine. The scholarly monograph, once the hallmark of academic achievement in the humanities and social sciences, has withered."

The increase in subscription fees presents a serious threat to library purchasing capability. And librarians are therefore frustrated since they cannot serve their campuses and communities sufficiently. Traditionally, single-copy purchasing of monographs and journals was adopted to cope with the increase in subscription fees. The situation is deteriorating because the percentage of the total serial universe held by member libraries of the Association of Research Libraries (ARL) dropped from 33% in 1973 to 26% in 1987 (Metz and Gherman, 1991). And it was projected that libraries will eventually only be able to purchase 2% of the total information (Hawkins, 1994).

There has been considerable backlash in the library and academic communities against commercial publishers in response to the increase in journal and monograph costs. The dilemma within the academic communities lies between the desire for publishing in peer-reviewed journals for academic promotion and the desire for self-publishing and self-archiving. However, as Keller (2001) states, "As long as journals remain the main indicator for quality control, scholars will be forced to publish in high-quality journals in order to enhance their career." Academic communities have worked out ways of resolving legitimacy in the print environment. Trust and legitimacy will continue to shape scholarly communication as we move from paper to electronic formats. Kling and McKim (2000) note that "it is likely that some conversions of scientific communication will change in the next decade, especially when they can be organized to preserve or enhance trust and bring other benefits as well."

The role of libraries in the evolving scholarly communication system will continue to be a central focus in the library and academic communities. As major changes in scholarly publishing continue to occur, "libraries and librarians will have new opportunities to participate in the evolving communications systems that will transform roles while at the same time preserving some of their traditional functions" (Crawford, Hurd and Weller, 1996).

New Role of Librarians

Researchers are overwhelmed by the explosive growth of scholarly production. This trend will likely be exacerbated by the vast amount of information on the Web. According to "Sizing the Internet: A Cyveillance Study" (2000), 7.3 million pages are added to the Web each day. The availability of information in a variety of formats and channels requires examination of how print and electronic resources are best served, and to understand how users make choices between library-provided materials and information available on the Web. Almost everyone is experiencing information overload today. In an information-abundant environment, the quality of information is more important than quantity. One important role of librarians is to educate the public about the value of library resources and to "help users select the best resources and overcome information overload" (Tenopir, 2003). Chapter 9 concentrates on the perceived advantages and limitations of digital and traditional libraries, and discusses the circumstances that affect the selection of use between electronic and print resources.

THE NEED FOR OLDER DOCUMENTS

In the digital age, whether older documents will be used or not has caught special attention in the library and information science community. King and his associates have produced a series of excellent studies on the trends in scholarly journals since the 1960s. In an article, "Designing Electronic Journals with 30 Years of Lessons from Print," Tenopir and King (1998) focus on the information-seeking patterns and their relevance with electronic publishing. Their survey reveals that 15% of articles read by university scientists and 11% by other scientists were more than five years old. The need for older information has implications for electronic publishing as well as for the design of digital libraries, since most of the older documents are not available in electronic formats. In his article "Electronic Journals: Why Do Users Think of Them?" McKnight (1997) notes that people used more than the current issues. The paucity of back issues of many electronic journals also implies that people still need to rely on physical libraries for older information. In a recent article on the digital library as place, Pomerantz and Marchionini (2007) write that "some non-digital materials may never have digital representations made of them, and some non-digital materials will always need to be accessed in their original forms for certain purposes. These materials must be stored and made accessible somewhere, so the authors suggest that the library and the archive will continue to be relevant for the foreseeable future."

According to Guthrie (2000), older documents seem to remain valuable in many fields. He finds that "the average age of the articles in the top ten most printed and viewed articles in the economics cluster is 13 years," and "an even more dramatic example is mathematics, where the average age of the most used articles in the field thus far is 32 years! This result is consistent with what mathematicians have told us about their field; that is, that older mathematics literature remains valuable."

Citation analysis has been employed as a reliable and measurable indicator of information use. A citation analysis of literature in computer science by Goodrum et al. (2001) reveals that even in computer science, people still used older documents extensively, as indicated by the age of the highly cited works. Their study concludes that "while there can be no doubt that the World Wide Web provides a fast and efficient means of disseminating and accessing scientific information, it may be premature to ring the death knell for traditional publishing and databases that provide access to the traditionally published literature."

To provide a sensitive yardstick for estimating the usage of old information, this section looks at how old documents are used in today's Internet age by analyzing citation data of the issues published in 2000. Citations represent documented evidence of information use. Ages of cited documents were measured by the years between the publication of citing articles and cited articles. For example, if an article published in 2000 cited an article published in 1995, then the age of the source document is counted as five years. Analyzing the distribution of ages of cited documents could provide us a better understanding for the design of electronic publishing systems as well as digital libraries. Since the *Journal of the American Chemical Society* published 1298 articles in 2000, it is impractical to analyze citation data of all these articles. In this

Table 3.5
Ages of Cited Documents in Chemistry

Ages of source documents	Number of references	Percentage
0–2 years old	110	21.7%
3–5 years old	140	27.6%
6–10 years old	91	17.9%
11–15 years old	57	11.2%
Over 15 years old	110	21.7%

Source: Journal of the American Chemical Society (2000).

section, only citation data of the first ten articles of these three journals were selected as source documents for analysis.

Generally speaking, current documents are more frequently used than older documents. As scholarly publishing and libraries are shifting from paper-based formats to electronic formats, new information is becoming widely available. But we should not forget that in the Internet age where new information is easily accessible, people are still using older documents. As indicated by the following three tables, the percentage of cited documents that are over fifteen years old (published before 1984) accounts for 21.7% in chemistry, 37.8% in mathematics, and 33.1% in sociology, respectively.

Some source documents in chemistry are over fifty years old. In mathematics and sociology, researchers cited documents that were published over 150 years before. One possible explanation is that old publications are often used for research purposes, and new articles may be used for casual interest and current awareness (Tenopir and King, 1998). The need for old information raises a challenge for electronic publishing and digital libraries. It also implies the need for digitizing older materials for future use. It is interesting to note here that when I collected data for this chapter, I still needed to go to libraries at the University of California at Berkeley to access dusty volumes that were published over 100 years ago. Tenopir and King (1998) note that "the danger is that, in the future, older articles will be ignored because they are not available electronically." It is unclear that people are still using old publications in the Internet age where new information is easily accessible. How to satisfy their needs for older documents is an important topic that deserves further exploration.

The distribution of ages of cited documents has important implications for the design of electronic publishing systems and digital libraries. The need for older documents implies that physical libraries can become primary sources of older publications, because of the paucity of back issues in many electronic journals. More importantly, there will be the hybrid of physical libraries and digital-only libraries in the future. Physical libraries and digital libraries will be mutually supported. In the age of digital libraries, physical libraries are very

Table 3.6
Ages of Cited Documents in Mathematics

Ages of source documents	Number of references	Percentage
0–2 years old	24	10.0%
3–5 years old	42	17.4%
6–10 years old	45	18.7%
11–15 years old	39	16.2%
Over 15 years old	91	37.8%

Source: American Journal of Mathematics (2000).

likely to play an indispensable role such as a repository of older publications and a "backup" function for preservation purposes.

The changing information environment requires libraries to reassess their roles and responsibilities in the digital era. Marcum (2003) points out that, "Preservation of books has been an important concern of librarians for decades, but the preservation of digital resources raises important and urgent issues. Books and manuscripts may be discovered decades after their publication and are still readable, even if the paper is fragile. Digital information, however, cannot be read in even a few years if the creator did not have the foresight to include information about the hardware and software used to create the content. For the first time, the decision to preserve must be made at the point of creation." It is possible that entire digital libraries would disappear if efforts are not made to maintain them. The responsibility of libraries in preservation would therefore rise to a new level of importance, given the fragility of digital media.

Libraries increasingly provide access to materials they do not own. Many libraries today have to depend on publishers not only to provide access to electronic resources, but also to archive them (Schaffner, 2001). Kuny (1997) states, "The archiving and preservation functions within a digital environment will become increasingly privatized as information continues to be commodified. Companies will be the place where the most valuable information is

Table 3.7
Ages of Cited Documents in Sociology

Ages of source documents	Number of references	Percentage
0–2 years old	52	6.6%
3–5 years old	144	18.3%
6–10 years old	196	25.0%
11–15 years old	133	16.9%
Over 15 years old	260	33.1%

Source: American Journal of Sociology (2000).

retained and preserved, and this will be done only insofar as there is a corporate recognition of the information as an asset. But companies have no binding commitment to making information available over a long-term.... Libraries will be the archive of last resort and will be repositories of ephemera and 'public domain' information—those materials considered as largely without commercial value." One important role of librarians and archivists in the digital environment is to continue to "protect the public interest by making information available to the community and by asserting the importance of maintaining a record of our collective intellectual heritage."

One of the grand challenges raised by the transition from a paper-based environment to a digital environment is how to preserve valuable digital records. The following chapter will take a closer look at issues related to digital preservation.

REFERENCES

Albanese, A.R. (2001). Revolution or Evolution: Trends in Electronic Scholarly Publishing. *Library Journal*, 126(18), 48–51.

Albee, B. and Dingley, B. (2001). U.S. Periodical Prices—2001. *American Libraries*, 32(5), 72–78.

Bordons, M. and Gomez, I. (2000). Collaboration Networks in Science. In B. Cronin and H.B. Atkins (Eds.), *The Web of Knowledge: A Festschrift in Honor of Eugene Garfield* (pp. 197–213). Medford, NJ: Information Today.

Broad, W.J. (1981). The Publishing Game: Getting More or Less. *Science*, 211(4487), 1137–1139.

Buckland, M.K. (1992). *Redesigning Library Services: A Manifesto*. Chicago, IL: American Library Association.

Cason, J.A. (1992). Authorship Trends in Poultry Science, 1981 through 1990. *Poultry Science*, 71(8), 1283–1291.

Constantian, M.B. (1999). The Gordian Knot of Multiple Authorship. *Plastic and Reconstructive Surgery*, 103(7), 2064–2066.

Crawford, S.Y., Hurd, J.M., and Weller, A.C. (1996). *From Print to Electronic: The Transformation of Scientific Communication*. Medford, NJ: Information Today.

Cronin, B. (2001). Hyperauthorship: A Postmodern Perversion or Evidence of a Structural Shift in Scholarly Communication Practices? *Journal of the American Society for Information Science and Technology*, 52(7), 558–569.

Darnton, R. (1989). Towards a History of Reading. *Wilson Quarterly*, 13(4), 87–102.

Drenth, J. (2001). Professors Responsible for Increasing in Authorship. *International Congress on Biomedical Peer Review and Scientific Publication*. Retrieved September 20, 2007, from http://www.ama-assn.org/public/peer/prau.htm.

Epstein, R.J. (1993). Six Authors in Search of a Citation: Villains or Victims of the Vancouver Convention? *British Medical Journal*, 306(6880), 765–767.

Goodrum, A.A., McCain, K.W., Lawrence, S., and Giles, C.L. (2001). Scholarly Publishing in the Internet Age: A Citation Analysis of Computer Science Literature. *Information Processing and Management*, 37(5), 661–675.

Guthrie, K.M. (2000). Revitalizing Older Published Literature: Preliminary Lessons from the Use of JSTOR. Retrieved January 29, 2008, from http://www.si. umich.edu/PEAK-2000/guthrie.pdf.

Hawkins, B.L. (1994). Creating the Library of the Future: Incrementalism Won't Get Us There! *The Serials Librarian*, 24(3–4), 17–47.

Keller, A. (2001). Future Development of Electronic Journals: A Delphi Survey. *The Electronic Library*, 19(6), 383–396.

Kling, R. and McKim, G. (2000). Not Just a Matter of Time: Field Differences and the Shaping of Electronic Media in Supporting Scientific Communication. *Journal of the American Society for Information and Technology*, 51(14), 1306–1320.

Koehler, W., Anderson, A.D., Dowdy, B.A., Fields, D.E., Golden, M., Hall, D., Johnson, A.C., Kipp, C., Ortega, L.L., Ripley, E.B., Roddy, R.L., Shaffer, K.B., Shelburn, S., and Wasteneys, C.D. (2000). A Bibliometric Exploration of the Demographics of Journal Articles: Fifty Years of *American Documentation* and the *Journal of the American Society for Information Science. CyberMetrics*, 4(1), Paper 3. Retrieved June 20, 2004, from http://www.cindoc.csic.es/ cybermetrics/articles/v4i1p3.html.

Kuny, T. (1997). The Digital Dark Ages? Challenges in the Preservation of Electronic Information. *63rd IFLA Council and General Conference*. Retrieved February 23, 2008, from http://www.ifla.org/IV/ifla63/63kuny1.pdf.

Lanham, R.A. (1997). The Economy of Attention. *Michigan Quarterly Review*, 36(2), 270–284.

Levy, D.M. (1997). I Read the News Today, Oh Boy: Reading and Attention in Digital Libraries. In *Proceedings of the 2nd ACM International Conference on Digital Libraries* (pp. 202–211). New York, NY: ACM Press.

Marcum, D.B. (2003). Research Questions for the Digital Era Library. *Library Trends*, 51(4), 636–651.

McDonald, K.A. (1995, April 28). Too Many Co-Authors? *Chronicle of Higher Education*, A35–A36.

McKnight, C. (1997). Electronic Journals: What Do Users Think of Them? In *Proceedings of International Symposium on Research, Development and Practice in Digital Libraries*. Tsukuba, Japan. Retrieved June 23, 2008, from http://www.dl.slis.tsukuba.ac.jp/ISDL97/proceedings/mcknight.html.

Metz, P. and Gherman, P.M. (1991). Serials Pricing and the Role of the Electronic Journal. *College & Research Libraries*, 52(4), 315–327.

Odlyzko, A.M. (1995). Tragic Loss or Good Riddance? The Impending Demise of Traditional Scholarly Journals. *International Journal of Human-Computer Studies*, 42(1), 71–122.

Pomerantz, J. and Marchionini, G. (2007). The Digital Library as Place. *Journal of Documentation*, 63(4), 505–533.

Price, D. (1965). *Little Science, Big Science*. New York, NY: Columbia University Press.

Sampson, Z.J. (1995). Authorship Counts: Forty years of the *Physical Review* and *Physical Review Letters. Scientometrics*, 32(2), 219–226.

Sandberg-Diment, E. (1987, March 15). The Execute Computer; How to Avoid Tunnel Version. *New York Times*. Retrieved February 28, 2008, from http://query.nytimes.com/gst/fullpage.html?res=9B0DEFDA1639F936A2 5750C0A961948260&sec=&spon=&pagewanted=1.

Schaffner, B.L. (2001). Electronic Resources: A Wolf in Sheep's Clothing. *College & Research Libraries*, 62(3), 239–249.

Sizing the Internet: A Cyveillance Study. (2000, July 10). *Cyveillance Press Release*. Retrieved July 22, 2001, from www.cyveillance.com.

Sobal, J. and Ferentz, K.S. (1990). Abstract Creep and Author Inflation. *New England Journal of Medicine*, 323(7), 488–489.

Tenopir, C. (2003). Electronic Publishing: Research Issues for Academic Librarians and Users. *Library Trends*, 51(4), 614–635.

Tenopir, C. and King, D.W. (1998). Designing Electronic Journals with 30 Years of Lessons from Print. *Journal of Electronic Publishing*, 4(2). Retrieved September 22, 2007, from http://www.press.umich.edu/jep/04-02/.

Tenopir, C. and King, D.W. (2004). *Communication Patterns of Engineers*. New York, NY: IEEE Press.

Wurman, R. (1989). *Information Anxiety*. New York, NY: Doubleday.

4

TRUST IN THE PRESERVATION OF DIGITAL INFORMATION

We live in a digital age. With an increasing amount of information being created, stored, and distributed in digital formats, preservation of digital information becomes a central concern as we embark on the digital society. Stille (2002) notes that "one of the great ironies of the information age is that, while the late twentieth century will undoubtedly have recorded more data than any other period in history, it will also almost certainly have lost more information than any previous era." Kuny (1997) points out that "Digital collections facilitate access, but do not facilitate preservation." He warns that we may be living in the midst of a digital dark ages due to the lack of concerted efforts for tackling problems in preserving our valuable cultural assets as well as personal digital belongings.

A recent wave of literature addresses issues of the preservation of digital media. Most previous studies focus on the fragility of digital media, technological obsolescence, and standards. Little attention has been given to the most critical barrier in the preservation of digital information: the potential conflicts between the new reality of digital information and the expectations of people. Deeply rooted in the context of "seeing is believing" of the printed

This chapter is an updated and expanded version of an earlier article: Hart, P. E. and Liu, Z. (2003). Trust in the Preservation of Digital Information. *Communications of the ACM*, 46(6), 93–97.

world, people's confidence tends to be directly linked to visibility, that is, people are confident in things that are tangible rather than intangible. Based on our survey of 110 people who have intensive experience in handling digital information, such as office workers, students, teachers, scientists, and administrators, we find that the major challenge in digital preservation is to increase people's confidence and trust in digital information. In this chapter, we attempt to apply "institutional guarantee," a concept derived from our analysis of currency, to the development of trusted systems for the preservation of digital information.[1] It begins with a detailed discussion on the new characteristics in the preservation of digital information, with particular attention given to underlying factors resulting in the low trust and confidence in digital preservation, then proceeds to the implications of paper and monetary currency, and finally puts forward suggestions for developing a widely trusted system.

NEW CHARACTERISTICS IN THE PRESERVATION
OF DIGITAL INFORMATION

The arrival of digital media not only offers new opportunities, but also poses unprecedented challenges. A major finding of our survey is that while individuals recognize the new opportunities offered by new digital media, they do not yet embrace them wholeheartedly.[2] For example, when we ask participants, "If you have an electronic copy of important documents, will you discard the paper documents," 95 of 110 (86%) respondents in our survey report they would not discard the paper documents. The five most common factors cited for not discarding paper documents include inaccessibility, lack of tangibility, fluidity, short preservation period, and concern about privacy and security.

Inaccessibility

Dependency and accessibility are the most commonly cited reasons for the lack of confidence and trust in preserving digital documents. Traditionally, a paper-based medium has been the dominant medium used for document recording, storage, distribution, and utilization. "[T]here is no compelling need to consider these as separate entities. There has also been no compelling need to distinguish between the format of a document and the medium in which it is embodied, since there is only one dominant choice of medium" (Lynn, 1995). The higher information density of digital media leads to the paradigm shift in the preservation practice: from preservation to access. Preserving digital information without making it accessible is simply a waste of effort. The dependence on equipment and software for preserving digital information potentially leads to inconvenience in accessing information and low trust and confidence in digital preservation. One respondent reports that "I preserved electronic copies of financial documents, and then had a hard disk crash. My fault for not having a backup." Another person in our survey notes, "Paper documents are more reliable. I can get to them in a power outage."

On the other hand, in order to achieve the requirements in accessing high-density digital media, we have to depend on reading devices that are rapidly becoming obsolescent (Conway, 1996; Rothenberg, 1995). People tend to cherish convenience and ignore any technology with characteristics that limit convenience (such as dependence on reading devices). "The electronic copies might disappear or fail to migrate to future technology," said one respondent. Another respondent points out that accessing electronic documents depends on too many variables. "Due to the rapid changes in hardware and software, there is no guarantee that the electronic documents will be accessible in the future."

Lack of Tangibility

"For the first time in 3,500 years of archival activity we produce records that do not exist to the human eye" (Cook, 1994). Information storage media have evolved toward greater information density, keeping the information operationally remote from the reader. Unlike information recorded on a paper-based medium, information on digital media is invisible to the human eye. However, deeply embedded in the context of "seeing is believing" of the printed culture for so many generations, people's confidence and trust in digital information is negatively associated with intangibility. Why should I trust something that is "invisible electromagnetic bumps on a plastic disk" clearly exemplifies this issue. One respondent comments, "I usually feel more comfortable having a paper copy of documents. And I feel more real." Another respondent reports: "It is still important to store the actual original documents."

Fluidity

Fixity is an inherent feature of paper documents, while fluidity comes with digital documents. The fluidity nature of digital information is reflected as follows: digital information is tentative and "work-in-progress," allowing continuous alteration; unlike the "stand-still" nature of a paper-based medium, digital information is "elusive," displaying on the screen and disappearing constantly; digital information is dynamic rather than static, which is even more apparent in hypertext and hypermedia (O'Toole, 1994). Spinellis (2002) finds that 41% of the URLs referenced in articles published in *Computer* and *Communications of the ACM* during 1995 and 1999 were no longer accessible by 2002.

One respondent mentions one important reason why he/she does not want to discard paper copies of important documents: "A paper copy is always the exact version you sent in somewhere. An electronic copy can be altered." Preserving something that can be easily altered clearly conflicts with our traditional perception of preservation. Conway (1996) notes that the term "archival" traditionally refers to "permanent" and preservation focused on infinity.

Short Preservation Period

In the evolution of document media, the physical life of document media, with a handful of exceptions, such as microfilm and WORM, tends to be shorter. Clay tablets and stone are not so easily destroyed; however, destroying digital information can be effortlessly done with a few keystrokes. The loss of information on highly acidic paper is gradual and partial; in contrast, the loss of information on digital media is always sudden and total. On the other hand, because of the fragility of digital media and the rapid obsolescence of reading devices, we cannot guarantee that digital information can be readable after ten years, let alone 500 years, which is a standard timeframe for the preservation of printed information. Traditionally, people tend to think of preservation periods in terms of centuries instead of a few years. This shift in preservation does have a far-reaching impact on preservation decisions. "Paper documents last longer," one respondent says. Another respondent points out, "Why should I preserve something that cannot be used within a decade. It is a waste of effort. Maybe we must wait for a better or cheaper technological solution." Similar findings have also been reported by Kimbrough's study (2004). Her survey reveals that cost of preservation is a deciding factor, given "the unpredictability of future spending on maintenance and equipment to support digitally preserved information." One librarian in her survey comments, "I would not want to spend scarce resources on a process that does not at this time have a long life." People may not adopt a technology until they feel it is stable. People's inertia to print media also plays a significant role. The conflict between rapid technological change and people's reluctance to respond can be another psychological barrier hindering the adoption of digital technologies for preservation. A report issued by the Electronic Resource Preservation and Access Network (2004) suggests that besides the fact that digital records are much more vulnerable than paper-based documents, people may not feel secure since they are not sure whether their procedures are effective or whether they can guarantee the authenticity and longevity of the digital objects for which they are responsible.

Privacy and Security

Privacy and security are concerns in preserving digital information. One respondent explains: "I did it once—entered addresses, phone numbers, birthdays, etc. in an electronic organizer . . . then the organizer was stolen and I no longer had the information." The growing worries about privacy and security are also confirmed by a report stressing, "remote storage is an advantage, security worries are a drawback" (Robinson, 1997).

Kimbrough (2004) finds that 80% of libraries in her survey express "concerns about digital preservation as a viable long term solution for law libraries." Distrust is a major concern for academic law libraries as they consider preservation questions. She notes: "While they overwhelmingly supported the preservation goals central to digitization, they remained skeptical about the process."

Obviously, many people have low confidence and trust in digital preservation. For example, few people today would throw away paper copies of important documents even if they have digital versions of exactly the same information. Fewer still would scan their paper documents into a digital storage system and then throw away the paper. However, as indicated by the following survey results, there is a need for preserving information electronically. When we ask, "If you have a paper copy of important documents, do you still want to preserve a digital copy of those important documents," only twenty-five of 110 respondents (23%) believe that they do not want to have an electronic copy of important documents. "A paper copy is enough. Why bother;" "if the paper copy is safe, like a birth certificate in a safety deposit box, there is no need for a digital copy." Ten of 110 people (9%) do not give a definite answer. One respondent mentions, "It depends on the energy and effort involved with preserving the digital copy." It is very interesting to find that seventy-five of 110 respondents (68%) in our survey report that they still want to preserve an electronic copy of important documents. Reasons for the need of having a digital copy include

- "It is easier to distribute electronic documents such as pictures to others;"
- "It is easier to edit, reorganize, or distribute;"
- "It's also sometimes easier to locate electronic files;"
- "Digital copy makes it easier to recreate or reuse the documents;"
- "As a backup in case of destruction or loss of paper documents;" and
- Keeping a digital copy "gives a feeling of security. If there is a fire, I might lose the paper documents. But if I have a digital copy, especially one stored off site, I should be OK."

PAPER, CURRENCY, AND THEIR IMPLICATIONS

We believe that the creation of an institutional guarantee for trusted digital preservation is instrumental to increasing people's confidence and trust in digital media, since there are no precursors for preserving documents of this nature. Unless people have sufficient confidence in digital documents (particularly in electronic representation of currency), as they have in paper and monetary currency, they will not trust electronic document management appliances. The relationship between confidence and institutional guarantee can be derived from the following analysis.

The Conventional View of the Role of Paper

Discussions of the merits of information on paper conventionally focus on the physical attributes of paper: creditability, light weight and not battery-dependence enables portability, high resolution and contrast make paper easier to read than screens, and so forth.

Suppose an ideal display medium could be developed that shares or approaches paper's physical advantages of weight, resolution, etc., would that lead to the replacement of paper by digital devices? For many purposes and in many contexts, no doubt it would. If the physical limitations of today's display devices could be overcome, then the many advantages of digital systems would be widely enjoyed. The conventionally mentioned advantages of digital presentations include the ability to search, edit, annotate, and transmit information.

But, what about the storage of information? Both, paper and digital devices can store as well as display information. If we were inclined to replace paper by digital devices because of a future ideal digital display medium, then we would also be replacing the storage function of paper by a digital storage function. Is this likely to happen? The answer is no, given current storage technology and systems. In other words, an ideal digital display medium is not by itself enough to cause "the end of paper."

Paper and Currency: In What Way Is Paper Like Currency?

What is currency? The economist's classical answer to the question "what is currency" is two fold: Currency is "a store of value," and currency is "a medium of exchange." A "store of value" means that currency, intrinsically, has value that is preserved over extended periods of time with no effort on the part of its owner. A "medium of exchange" means that the exchange of currency is the way that economic transactions are performed.

How is paper like currency? Paper shares two fundamental properties with currency. From an information–theoretic point of view, paper carries two similar connotations: (1) it is "a store of information" and (2) it is "a medium of *direct* exchange of information with a person." A "store of information" means especially the information is preserved over an extended period of time with no effort on the part of its owner. A "medium of *direct* exchange" means that a producer of paper-based information can provide that information directly to a consumer of information without using any type of device or intermediary. "Consume" information certainly means reading it, but we can also include operations like annotation if we agree that pencils are trivial "devices."

Why Digital Information Is Not Like Paper (or Currency)?

Information in digital systems—even in digital systems with an ideal and paper-like display medium—is not like paper-based information because (1) information is not preserved over an extended period of time with no effort on the part of its owner, and (2) the information cannot be consumed without the use of a nontrivial device.

A key point in this discussion is the meaning of "extended period of time." What does "extended" mean? It is possible to read Babylonian clay tablets and Egyptian papyrus created a few millennia ago, if you understand the language or symbols. It is possible to read, say, English documents printed a few centuries ago. But who among us can "read" electronic documents that were stored on digital media only a few decades ago? Do you still have your 8-inch floppy drive? Will the mainframe tapes melt or ignite when spun on drives that are ten times faster than they were only twenty years ago? And, of course, assuming the physical media can be read, is your software compatible with the old file formats?

People Do Not Trust Digital Information, But Why Do People Trust Electronic Representation of Currency?

Money has been viewed as a social contract. Aristotle stresses that money "exists not by nature but by law and it is in our power to change it and make it useless" (Lagerspetz, 1984). The appearance of paper currency made the contract theory of money more appealing than before, where monetary institutions are viewed as being based on an explicit social contract.

Initially, currency had intrinsic value because of the form or material of which it was composed. Whether the seashells of coastal people that were passed inland from hand-to-hand, or the gold pieces of mercantilist Europeans, currency per se originally had perceived value. Later, paper currency gained acceptance as a surrogate for metallic currency (you may remember the long-gone "Silver Certificate" dollar bills issued by the U.S. treasury), though there have been many times and places in history where paper currency came to have little or no value. And finally, electronic representations of currency gained wide acceptance—we accept the bank balance printed out for us by the automatic teller machine without questioning, "where actually is the real currency?"

What lies behind this willingness to accept surrogates in place of "the real thing?" Clearly, institutional guarantees are central to the process. Whether it was paper currency issued by a private bank in the era of Andrew Jackson or the Federal Reserve today, most of us have to a greater or lesser extent been willing to accept that a trusted institution stood behind the value of the surrogate (though a few untrusting souls even today keep metallic coins under their mattresses). Then, is it possible to have institutional guarantees for the preservation of digital information? The answer could and should be yes.

DIGITAL MEDIA AND TRUST

The topic of "trust" has been discussed in a wide-range of disciplines, notably psychology, sociology, economics, management, and communications (Ebert, 2007). Trust is a fundamental concept. It is pervasive to every aspect of our daily life. Trust is not only a vital commodity, but also a fragile commodity. As trust declines, people are increasingly unwilling to take risks, demanding greater protections against possible failures, and resulting in slow adoption of new technologies. The lack of confidence and the need for trust may form a vicious circle (Gambetta, 1998). Low trust may result in failure to gain critical mass to sustain new business.

The cost of electronically storing documents is dipping below the cost of storing paper documents containing the same information. Yet, digital document management systems have enjoyed only a modest market penetration, and even then in rather specialized organizational settings—and none, whatsoever, in the small offices and home offices (SOHO) market. The lack of confidence and trust in digital information clearly results in retarding acceptance of digital preservation and electronic document management systems.

We believe that trust is instrumental for the preservation of digital media for the following reasons:

- Trust has to be achieved through a familiar world. Practices of preserving paper-based documents are relatively well developed. However, lack of experience raises concerns about how we should proceed with digital-based preservation (Jantz and Giarlo, 2005). We believe that one of the major reasons why people are not confident in digital preservation is that it is a new practice and people are not familiar with it. Confidence and trust may increase through use (Gambetta, 1998). With the continued penetration of digital media and development of related technologies, people will be more confident in digital preservation. Distrust is risk-averse while trust is risk-accepting phenomena. With more confidence in digital preservation, people may be willing to become "risk-taking" instead of being "risk-averse."

- Trust is linked to a given condition. Trusting behavior changes as document medium changes. The transition from the preservation of paper media to digital media may have the same consequences.

- Trust requires accountability and tangibility. People may not trust things that are intangible and unaccountable.

- Trust and scale are dynamically intertwined. People may not trust a digital preservation system operated by a small company or dominated by a single big corporation. However, people may trust a digital preservation operated by a consortium of many industries and organizations, or a network of trusted institutions. On the other hand, lack of trust may result in the withdrawal of activities and prevent early adoption of new technology. Through lack of trust, a system may lose size and fail to achieve "critical mass" to sustain the business (Fukuyama, 1995).

- Trust is not only critical for the users of digital preservation, but also for the players in digital preservation. Trust is at the heart of forming partnerships across institutions. Trust develops through experience, reputation, and accreditation. New business requires risk taking, and risk taking requires trust. The lack of confidence and the need for trust in the preservation of digital media may form a vicious circle.

Lynch (1994) notes, "We are somewhat vague about what we expect, and we do not always understand what a given system can actually do. Our lack of clarity produces both overly optimistic (trusting) and overly pessimistic perceptions. In the world of digital information, the tools and mechanisms of ensuring integrity are complex and exotic, and our unfamiliarity with these tools leads us to distrust their efficacy."

According to the National Science Foundation/Joint Information Systems Committee (NSF/JISC) Repositories Workshop, the development of trust mechanisms is crucial to long-term sustainability in digital preservation. However, many related issues remain unsolved such as "how can accountability be built into trust agreements," "what are the reasonable expectations from providers, partners, and users," "what are the appropriate methods for testing trust," and "what happens when trust relationships are broken" (Berman, McDonald, Schottlaender and Kozbial, 2007). Answering these questions will prove critical as we attempt to ensure long-term access to digital assets.

The more pervasive the digital information, the more critical trust becomes. We need a kind of institutional guarantee mechanism that the integrity of digital information will be preserved and that it will remain retrievable and readable. The Center for Art and Media (ZKM) in Karlsruhe, Germany is creating an international network of scalable, open system-based archives, powerful enough to manage heritage collections. The idea of "institutional guarantee" seems to have been applied to digital preservation. Cornwell and Shintani (2005) report the pilot implementation of "institutional guarantee" and note that "Historically, examples of institutional guarantee include the introduction of symbolic financial instruments, such as paper banknotes. Underlying distributed computer networks is the fact that multiple distributed copies of important media holdings are evidently more secure than two or even three conventional tape archives. Because identical master copies of titles can be maintained securely on a geographically distributed computer network, individual installations might be attacked without impact upon the safety of actual collections. Security of title masters is guaranteed through the automated maintenance of archive mirrors at several locations, and in turn, institutions and curators of exhibitions gain new possibilities of collection sharing." They add: "In a first demonstration of 'institutional guarantee', two major institutions have joined forces utilizing ZKM's Digital Heritage system. By mid-2005, the Netherlands Media Art Institute, Montevideo/Time Based Arts and the Science Museum London will share cloned copies of parts of their collections."

GENERIC TRUST REQUIREMENTS FOR DIGITAL PRESERVATION

The Stanford Digital Repository (SDR) focuses on maintaining integrity, authenticity, and readability of digital information over time. A proposal, *"Designing Digital Preservation Repository Services at Stanford,"* clearly states that "the most important function of any service designed for the long term is building and nurturing trust—maintaining the trust of its depositors is the SDR's foremost priority."

The application of trust in computer systems originated in the 1970s with a special emphasis on software and security issues. The trustworthiness of digital objects depends on what happens to them and by whom they are preserved. We believe that trust needs to be embraced in every component and process included in the preservation of digital information. For example, these include trusted people (e.g., trusted skills and behaviors), trusted process and procedure (e.g., protections and controls against loss), trusted media, trusted hardware and software, trusted network, trusted management (e.g., policy and regulations), and trusted insurance mechanism.

Preservation of digital information is an extremely complex issue. No single organization can effectively deal with it. Instrumental in building trust in digital preservation is an institutional guarantee mechanism through the participation of a multitude of players, including content producers; the hardware, software, and telecommunications industries; document companies; the insurance industry; public certified agencies; and professional organizations.

For example, digital documents (such as banking and insurance records) hold crucial financial and legal information. Unlike paper-based documents, information in digital documents can be easily altered. In order to cope with the fluidity of digital information, a "witness" or "notary public," or an independent certified agency is critical to an institutional guarantee mechanism of the integrity of digital documents (Lynch, 1994; Stornetta, 1995). Since preservation of digital information is young and maturing, the participation of professional organizations would help to provide guidelines regarding digital preservation.

Of course, different types of information and different purposes of preservation pose different requirements for institutional guarantees. The telecommunications industry will play an important role in online data backup; public-certified agencies would be indispensable for storage of fixed digital documents (such as banking, financial, and insurance records); document companies play a unique part in the "scanning-filing-storing-printing" of digital documents. The hardware and software industries can take care of renting and selling equipment and software to those who want to keep and retrieve confidential information by themselves.

Here's an old example: Around the turn of the last century Kodak offered a combined camera and development services built around the slogan, "You press the button, we do the rest." The camera was not "user-serviceable," came sealed with the film already installed, and after exposing the roll the entire unit was shipped to Kodak for developing and printing. We can approach digital preservation in the same way, perhaps with the slogan, "You send us the sealed CD/RW drive, we do the rest" (only if you have no Internet connection, of course). But if we took this idea seriously, then we might conclude that no single vendor has the credibility required. Instead, it might ultimately be necessary to form a kind of industry consortium that backed the document-integrity guarantee. Is this possible? Would it be in the commercial interests of today's leading companies to enter such an alliance, or would it be too severe a threat to existing paper-based businesses? In the latter case, is it possible that a new industry might some day arise that provides such a warranty? Are there parallels to these ideas of jointly guaranteeing some results in, for example, the insurance industry?

CONCLUSION

The cost of electronically storing documents is dipping below the cost of storing paper documents containing the same information. As of 2003, the marginal cost of disk space for storing a document page image is approaching 150 times less than the cost of the paper on which the document is printed, a huge gap that continues to widen. The cost and convenience advantages of digital archiving are compelling, but realizing the full benefits requires solutions to an issue as old as humanity and as new as the "next next thing," that is, trust.

NOTES

1. Trust in digital preservation has been extensively discussed. See, for example, Ross and McHugh (2006) and RLG/OCLC Working Group on Digital Archive Attributes (2002). The purpose of that paper was not to tackle the specific problems identified in the Research Libraries Group's report (Marshall and Golovchinsky, 2004). Rather, from a management and policy's perspective, it argues that an institutional guarantee mechanism can help address the major hurdle—regaining people's confidence and trust in the digital preservation environment, since there are no precursors for preserving documents of this nature.

2. How was the survey conducted? The survey was designed to examine people's perceptions and confidence in digital preservation. Survey questions include: What types of digital documents do you want to preserve? If you have an electronic copy of important documents, do you want to discard the paper documents? In what cases will you discard the paper documents and keep the digital documents? If you have a paper copy of important documents, do you still want to preserve a digital copy of those important documents? We also asked for reasons. Participating in this survey are people with extensive experience in handling electronic information, such as students, teachers, scientists, engineers, and office workers. One hundred and eighty questionnaires were distributed in 2001; we received 110 completed responses and seven incomplete ones.

REFERENCES

Berman, F., McDonald, R.H., Schottlaender, B., and Kozbial, A. (2007). *The Need for Formalized Trust in Digital Repository Collaborative Infrastructure.* Retrieved February 22, 2008, from http://www.sis.pitt.edu/~repwkshop/papers/berman_schottlaender.html.

Conway, P. (1996). *Preservation in the Digital World.* Washington, DC: Commission on Preservation and Access.

Cook, T. (1994). *It's 10 O'clock: Do You Know Where You Data Are?* Retrieved February 22, 2008, from http://web.mit.edu/erm/tcook.tr1995.html.

Cornwell, P. and Shintani, J. (2005). *Conservation-Quality Digital Media Systems and Distributed Archives.* Retrieved October 15, 2007, from http://jim2005.mshparisnord.org/download/26.%20Shintani.pdf.

Designing Digital Preservation Repository Services at Stanford: Practical Theory for Practical Services. Retrieved February 22, 2008, from http://www.cni.org/tfms/2006a.spring/abstracts/handouts/CNI_Designing_Johnson.doc.

Ebert, T. (2007). *Interdisciplinary Trust Meta-Analysis: Analysis of High Rank Trust Articles between 1966 and 2006.* Ludwig-Maximilians-Universität München Munich School of Management. Retrieved February 22, 2008, from http://epub.ub.uni-muenchen.de/1388/1/20070613_LMU_Disskussionsbeitraege_Trust.pdf.

Electronic Resource Preservation and Access Network (2004). *The Role of Audit and Certification in Digital Preservation.* Retrieved February 22, 2008, from http://www.erpanet.org/events/2004/antwerpen/Workshop_Antwerpen_report.pdf.

Fukuyama, F. (1995). *Trust: The Social Virtues and the Creation of Property.* New York, NY: Free Press.

Gambetta, D. (1998). *Trust: Making and Breaking Cooperative Relations.* New York, NY: Basil Blackwell.

Jantz, R. and Giarlo, M. (2005). Digital Preservation: Architecture and Technology for Trusted Digital Repositories. *D-Lib Magazine*, 11(6). Retrieved October 20, 2007, from http://www.dlib.org/dlib/june05/jantz/06jantz.html.

Kimbrough, J.L. (2004). *21st Century Preservation Challenges for Law Libraries.* MSLS Thesis, University of North Carolina at Chapel Hill, United States. Retrieved October 20, 2007, from http://etd.ils.unc.edu:8080/dspace/bitstream/1901/34/1/juliekimbrough.pdf.

Kuny, T. (1997). The Digital Dark Ages? Challenges in the Preservation of Electronic Information. *63rd IFLA Council and General Conference.* Retrieved October 20, 2007, from http://www.ifla.org/IV/ifla63/63kuny1.pdf.

Lagerspetz, E. (1984). Money As a Social Contract. *Theory and Decision*, 17(1), 1–9.

Lynch, C.A. (1994). The Integrity of Digital Information: Mechanics and Definitional Issues. *Journal of the American Society for Information Science*, 45(10), 737–744.

Lynn, M.S. (1995). *Preservation and Access Technology.* Washington, DC: Commission on Preservation and Access.

Marshall, C.C. and Golovchinsky, G. (2004). Saving Private Hypertext: Requirements and Pragmatic Dimensions for Preservation. *Proceedings of ACM Hypertext 2004* (pp. 130–138). New York, NY: ACM Press.

O'Toole, J.M. (1994). On the Idea of Uniqueness. *American Archivist*, 57(4), 632–657.

RLG/OCLC Working Group on Digital Archive Attributes (2002). *Trusted Digital Repositories: Attributes and Responsibilities*. Retrieved October 20, 2007, from http://www.rlg.org/longterm/repositories.pdf.

Robinson, P. (1997, August 31). Online Data Backup Has Its Pros, Cons. *San Jose Mercury News*, 4F.

Ross, S. and McHugh, A. (2006). The Role of Evidence in Establishing Trust in Repositories. *D-Lib Magazine*, 12(7/8). Retrieved October 20, 2007, from http://www.dlib.org/dlib/july06/ross/07ross.html.

Rothenberg, J. (1995). Ensuring the Longevity of Digital Documents. *Scientific American*, 272(1), 42–47.

Spinellis, D. (2002). The Decay and Failures of Web References. *Communications of the ACM*, 46(1), 71–77.

Stille, A. (2002). Are We Losing Our Memory? or the Museum of Obsolete Technology. In *The Future of the Past* (299). New York, NY: Farrar, Straus and Giroux. Retrieved October 23, 2007, from http://www.lostmag.com/issue3/memory.php.

Stornetta, W.S. (1995). Preserving the Integrity of Business Records in the Age of Electronic Commerce. *Computer Technology Review*, 10 (special supplement).

5

READING BEHAVIOR IN THE DIGITAL ENVIRONMENT

The impact of digital media on reading has increasingly been the object of empirical and theoretical exploration by researchers from a wide range of disciplines, notably psychology, computer science, education, literacy studies, and library and information science. Each discipline has developed its unique research focuses and methodology.[1]

With the growing amount of digital information available and the increasing amount of time people spend on reading electronic media, the digital environment has begun to affect people's reading behavior. A number of scholars argue that the arrival of digital media together with the fragmentary nature of hypertext is threatening sustained reading (Birkerts, 1994; Healy, 1990). Birkerts (1994) further notes that the younger generation growing up in the digital environment lacks the ability to read deeply and to sustain a prolonged engagement in reading.

Bolter (1991) states: "The shift from print to the computer does not mean the end of literacy itself, but the literacy of print, for electronic technology offers us a new kind of book and new ways to write and read." Digital media contribute to a transformative shift in reading. They also introduce a number of powerful advantages that are traditionally absent in the print environment, such as interactivity, nonlinearity, immediacy of accessing information, and the convergence of text, images, audio, and video (Landow, 1992; Lanham, 1993; Murray, 1997; Ross, 2003). Lanham (1995) compares the difference

---

This chapter is an updated and expanded version of an earlier article: Liu, Z. (2005). Reading Behavior in the Digital Environment: Changes in Reading Behavior over the Past 10 Years. *Journal of Documentation*, 61(6), 700–712.

between print literacy and digital literacy. He asserts that "In the world of print, the idea and its expression are virtually one. The meaning takes the form of words; words generate the meaning. Digital literacy works in an inherently different way. The same digital code that expresses words and numbers can, if the parameters of expression are adjusted, generate sounds and images. This parametric variation stands at the center of digital expressivity, a role it could never play in print." Digital literacy could potentially enhance our ability to make information more suitable to a targeted recipient (e.g., persons with disabilities). Whether people like digital media or not, reading and literacy is being redefined by the arrival of digital technology. The introduction of new media brings both positive and negative possibilities. In a study of the impact of new media on people's reading habits between 1970s and 1990s, Knulst and other researchers (1996) find that "the new media require users to articulate their preferences more explicitly. . . . Using a control panel, the user can impose his will down to the smallest detail, and is thus confronted each time with the results of his own preferences. In multimedia-land people are not encouraged to wait until they know more about a subject before they click on to the next, or to open themselves up to unknown points of view. And this is precisely one of the great achievements of the reading culture."

Print media and digital media have their own advantages and limitations. The challenge is to determine the applicability of a particular medium in a given context or process. For example, electronic media tend to be more useful for searching, while paper-based media are preferred for actual consumption of information.

Reading is still the most efficient method for communicating words. A more complex society will demand increased rather than decreased reading. The remaining question we should deal with is the medium through which reading is done. It seems unlikely that the computer in the future will replace the printed book as a reading medium in the way that it replaced the typewriter as a writing tool. Marshall (2005) notes that "reading is a heterogeneous activity and reading technologies are better for some things than they are for others. Choosing a single platform to support reading and critical thinking is not only unnecessary, it seems unlikely." Ross (2003) suggests that we need to pay more attention to how readers actually engage different media, their reason for choosing one format over another, and their satisfaction with each format.

In a recent study of reading practices at the National University of Mexico, Ramirez (2003) finds that nearly 80% of students prefer to read a digital piece of text in print in order to understand the text with clarity. Nearly 68% of the respondents report that they understand and retain more information when they read print media. However, only 4% of the respondents report the opposite. Lower resolution on a computer monitor is one of the major factors that people print out documents (especially lengthy documents) for reading. Recent studies show that reading from a monitor is up to 30% slower than reading the same text on a printed page (AlShaali and Varshney, 2005; Hartzell,

2002). Murphy and other researchers (2003) focus on the persuasiveness of printed and electronic texts. They note that undergraduate students, who read online text, find it more difficult to understand, less interesting, and the authors less credible than those who read text's printed version.

Adler and others (1998) describe work-related document (printed and electronic) activities of fifteen people from a variety of professions over a period of five consecutive working days. They find that document-activity time accounted for an average of nearly 82% of working time, ranging from 23% (for nurses) to 94% (the accounting assistant). A study of the document activities in the International Monetary Fund (IMF), a document-intensive organization, finds that 51% of document activities involves paper only, 14% involves digital documents only, and 35% a combination of paper and digital documents. Paper is superior to digital technologies for certain tasks such as reviewing the work of others, thinking and planning, meeting, and telephone activity (Sellen and Harper, 1997; 2002). Marshall (2005) also reports that paper documents still provide vital support for some document-related activities, even though it is no longer the sole viable reading medium. Clearly, there will be a coexistence of paper and digital documents in the future, simply because each medium tends to support certain activities that are not easily replaced by the other.

Reading is not a single activity. It is a complex and variable behavior. It involves different purposes and requires different skills in handling documents. McKnight (1997) offers a number of excellent insights in reading behavior of electronic media. He observes that people don't like to read from screens. They prefer to print out electronic documents for reading, even printouts from dot matrix printers. He argues that the trend in mounting electronic documents in Adobe's portable document format (pdf) also discourages screen reading and encourages printing. People tend to print out documents that are longer than can be displayed on a few screens. People also know how to organize and manipulate paper documents, but manipulating electronic documents requires a different set of skills.

People like to browse and find things by accident. Nunberg (1993) notes: "Browsing a document database will never be quite as informative as browsing a bookstore or library stacks, since electronic documents don't bear physical traces of their provenance the way print books do—the price we pay for delivering them of their bodies. But it may not be much different from browsing around in a video rental outlet." Olsen's study (1994) finds that serendipity was identified as an important factor by 82% of people in her survey.

Flipping and scanning (a reading pattern associated with printed documents) is not only a means for locating information in a document, but also a means to get a sense of the whole text. Scrolling on a computer screen does not support this mode of reading and information processing. Readers tend to establish a visual memory for the location of items on a page and within a document. Scrolling weakens this relationship (Olsen, 1994). This reading pattern has a historical analogy. As Manguel (1996) notes: "The unwieldy scroll possessed a limited surface—a disadvantage we are keenly aware of today, having returned to this ancient book form [codex] on our computer screens, which reveal only a portion of text at a time as we 'scroll' upwards or downwards."

In summary, the digital environment has begun to affect how people read. However, few studies have explored this fundamental issue. Researchers are only at the very early stage of discovering changes in reading patterns. Many previous studies attempt to explore reading in the digital environment by examining the evolution of reading or observing how people read documents (especially electronic documents) within a specific period of time. While these approaches are useful in discovering how reading behavior changes, they are limited. For example, the evolution approach allows us to see changes in reading from a historical perspective, but is limited in providing us with detailed information on how reading activities are actually changing. On the contrary, the observation approach gives us a detailed analysis and description of how people actually read, but fails to provide a broad picture of how reading behavior changes in the digital environment. This chapter attempts to explore reading in the digital environment from a different perspective. Instead of observing how people read electronic documents, this study attempts to investigate how people's reading behavior has changed over the past decade by self-reported measures of their overall reading experiences (including work-related reading and leisure reading).

A cluster of seventeen questions was designed to capture various dimensions of online reading behavior.[2] Participants were asked to respond to the following questions based on their overall reading experience over the past decade:[3]

- Time spent on reading.
- Percentage of time spent on reading printed documents.
- Percentage of time spent on reading electronic documents.
- Percentage of time spent on browsing and scanning.
- Percentage of time spent on key word spotting.
- Percentage of time spent on in-depth reading.
- Percentage of time spent on concentrated reading.
- Percentage of documents read one time (one-time reading).
- Reading things selectively.
- Nonlinear reading (e.g., jump).
- Sustained attention.
- Frequency of annotating printed documents while reading.
- Frequency of annotating electronic documents while reading.
- Frequency of highlighting printed documents while reading.

- Frequency of highlighting electronic documents while reading.
- Frequency of printing out electronic documents for reading.
- Preference for document media when reading.

TIME SPENT ON READING

In the digital age, people are spending more time on reading. Even though the amount of time spent on reading is highly related to work and family responsibilities, 67% of the participants in this survey report that they spend more time on reading, with about one-third of the participants indicating no change in reading time (see Table 5.1). Two major factors can contribute to the increase in reading time: information explosion and digital technology. Digital documents are easy to search, and also allow more opportunities for accessing more information. For example, a document on the Web has an average of nine links (Almind and Ingwersen, 1997). This means that when a user accesses a Web document, he/she at the same time has a chance of accessing nine other documents. Another problem that needs to be noted here is that people are confronted with the sheer volume and variety of information. How much time they choose to spend on reading is a very important decision, given the fact that they cannot increase the time on reading infinitely.

As indicated by Table 5.1, the majority (83%) of participants in this survey report that the percentage of time devoted to read electronically is increasing. This finding is quite consistent with other studies and statistics. The arrival of digital media has changed how we spend a significant portion of our time reading digital documents, time that otherwise would have been spent reading printed documents. According to the *United States Statistical Abstracts*, the total expense on print media is shrinking, while the total expenditure on electronic media is increasing. The trend in the growing consumption of electronic media and shrinking expenses on print media is further supported by the fact that more time is spent on online/Internet access and less time on conventional daily newspapers and consumer magazines.

Table 5.1
Time Spent on Reading

Changes	Time on reading	Time on reading electronic documents
More time	67.3%	83.2%
Less time	0%	10.6%
No change	31.9%	0.9%
Don't know	0.9%	5.3%
Total	100.1%	100.0%

Note: Figures of this and other tables may not add to 100% because of rounding.

SCREEN-BASED READING

The increasing mechanization of print facilitated a shift from intensive reading to extensive reading. Around 1750 there was a dramatic change in the way people read documents. Before this time, people were reading *intensively*. They had only a few books to read and they read them over and over again. By the early 1800s, however, people started to read things *extensively*. They read all kinds of material, especially periodicals and newspapers, and moved through one item after another (Darnton, 1989). From the evolution of reading, it is not difficult to imagine that browsing or scanning is becoming a principal reading pattern in today's information-intensive environment. With an increasing amount of time spent on reading electronic documents, the screen-based reading behavior is emerging. The screen-based reading behavior is characterized by more time on browsing and scanning, keyword spotting, one-time reading, nonlinear reading, and reading more selectively; while less time on in-depth reading, concentrated reading, and decreasing sustained attention (see Table 5.2).

One participant notes: "I skim much more html [hypertext markup language] pages than I do with printed materials." Another participant admits: "I don't have the patience to read page by page. I just like to skim around the text in order to find the most salient information." Changes in reading behavior are not only driven by information explosion and the arrival of digital media but also by social forces. Michie (1996) states that "fewer and fewer people now shift greater and greater workloads, driven ever faster by competitive anxieties, accentuated by rapid-creation interoffice and worldwide computer nets. The signs of competitive anxiety can already be observed in the workplace—shrinking attention span, abbreviation of working memory, top-of-the-head response, increasing emotionality, weakening of deliberative, deductive and ruminative thought, and aversion to the written word other than to scan it, annotate and pass it on."

Table 5.2
Screen-Based Reading Behavior

Percentage of time Spent on	Increasing	Decreasing	No change	Don't know
Browsing and scanning	80.5%	11.5%	8.0%	0%
Keyword spotting	72.6%	2.7%	16.0%	8.8%
One-time reading	56.6%	8.0%	29.2%	6.2%
Reading selectively	77.9%	2.7%	16.8%	2.7%
Nonlinear reading	82.3%	0%	15.9%	1.8%
Sustained attention	15.9%	49.6%	29.2%	5.3%
In-depth reading	26.6%	45.1%	23.0%	5.3%
Concentrated reading	21.2%	44.2%	26.5%	8.0%

More Browsing/Scanning and Keyword Spotting

As indicated in Table 5.2, over 80% of the participants in this survey report a greater percentage of time spent on browsing and scanning. A study of 350 scientific journals published over forty years (1944–1988) reveals "experimental results increasingly being foregrounded in titles, abstracts, introduction, and section headings, but methods and procedures sections increasingly being relegated to secondary status" (Berkenkotter and Huckin, 1993). Because of the growing number of scientific journals and the expansion of their volumes, readers of scientific journals cannot keep pace with the literature and are forced to skim journal articles the way that many readers skim newspapers. This trend tends to be more intensified in the Web environment. Most people tend to read the first screen of text only. Ninety percent of people reading a Web page don't scroll down (Goldsborough, 2000). Scanning offers an effective way to filter through the vast amount of information. On the other hand, scanning decreases learning (Eveland and Dunwoody, 2001). One participant points out: "I find that my patience with reading long documents is decreasing. I want to skip ahead to the end of long articles." Another participant reports that younger people do not have patience to read every word. They merely skim and look for needed information while reading. According to a study by Poynter Institute (2000), Web users tend to "do a lot of brief scanning, foraging quickly through many article summaries, but when their interest is caught they will dive into a particular topic or article in depth."

Over 72% of the respondents report more keyword spotting in their reading. It seems very likely that people employ keyword spotting as a strategy to locate needed information as a way to cope with the overloaded information environment. "People are doing more and more 'picture' reading, looking for illustrations to explain charts and pictures. Any document with texts only will bore many savvy IT users," noted one participant.

Birkerts (1996) stresses: "In our culture, access is not a problem, but proliferation is. And the reading act is necessarily different than it was in its earliest days. Awed and intimidated by the availability of texts, faced with the all but impossible task of discriminating among them, the reader tends to move across surfaces, skimming, hastening from one site to the next without allowing the words to resonate inwardly." As a result, we "know countless more 'bits' of information, both important and trivial, than our ancestors."

Increasing One-Time Reading and Selective Reading

Over 56% of the respondents note that the percentage of documents they read one time (one-time reading) is increasing. Since time devoted to reading is limited and they cannot keep pace with the growth of information production, this means that a smaller percentage of documents will be read (see also Chapter 3). On the other hand, a greater percentage of documents will be read only one time. According to Gordon (1997), 85% of printed documents are never referred to again.

Approximately 78% of the participants report they read more selectively. One respondent notes: "I would describe the information overload as drinking from a fire hose. I need to learn how to ignore things that are not highly relevant to my life." In the information-abundant world, attention becomes a scare resource. People tend to be more selective when they face an overwhelming amount of information. We cannot afford to pay attention to every single piece of information simply because it is there (Levy, 1997). We have to allocate our attention more selectively. In a search for relevant information, readers tend to exhibit more frequent and more overt selectivity, which in turn leads to both more partial and deeper understanding (Topping, 1997).

Increasing Nonlinear Reading and Declining Sustained Attention

Time spent on nonlinear reading is increasing, as reported by over 82% of the participants in this survey. And nearly half of the respondents in this study mention declining sustained attention in reading (see Table 5.2). Some participants mention that they dislike the loss of the sense of linearity in the online environment. One respondent mentions that jumping around through different links, and grabbing bits and pieces by navigating to different pages is certainly a different but also an exhaustive experience.

In the print environment, the text is fixed and the author determines the order in which ideas are presented. In hypertext, however, the author provides options, but readers choose the order through activating links (Ross, 2003). The arrival of hypertext enables more nonlinear reading (e.g., jump). Hyper-reading may also affect sustained attention and contributes to more fragmented reading, since each page has to compete with many other pages for a user's attention. Birkerts (1994) and Stoll (1995) note that the digital environment tends to encourage people to explore many topics extensively, but at a more superficial level. Hyperlinks distract people from reading and thinking deeply about a single subject. In a study of readers who read either a stimulated literacy hypertext or the same text in linear form, Miall and Dobson (2001) also find that "hypertext discourages the absorbed and reflective mode that characterizes literacy reading." Thirunarayanan (2003) observes that "if a Web page does not load within three seconds, people click their way to another Web page or site. Clicking is fast becoming a substitute for thinking. Clicking requires less effort than thinking and is in some instances less painful than thinking."

Decreasing In-Depth and Concentrated Reading

Eveland and Dunwoody (2001) find that it is very difficult for readers to devote full attention to reading because they have to decide which text to read, which hyperlink to follow, and whether to scroll down a page. Shallower and less in-depth reading is another feature of "hyper-extensive" reading.

While people today spend more time reading than they did in the print-only past, the depth and concentration associated with reading has declined. As shown in Table 5.2, about 45% of the participants in this study indicate that they are facing decreasing in-depth reading and concentrated reading. One participant notes: "It is hard to concentrate on reading documents on the Web. I need to learn how to ignore distracting colorful or blinking graphics. Having to continually close unwanted pop-up windows is also very distracting."

Some participants mention that their reading concentration is interrupted by other tasks (e.g., e-mail) when multiple windows are open. "I have to admit that my attention definitely decreased when I read online. I checked my fantasy football scores and stock quotes, surfed favorite news sites, and listened for the ping of e-mail from a particular response I was expecting," reported one participant. Since people are so connected, they no longer exist in their own space (Birkerts, 1994). Another respondent points out: "My attention while reading online is tempted by sudden recollection of Web sites I intend to visit and multi e-mail accounts that need to be checked. It is hard to concentrate on one thing until the end of semester is approaching."

Many people, especially younger ones, tend to work simultaneously on several tasks with multiple windows open. David Meyer finds that people who engage in multitasking behaviors, such as switching back and forth between the two tasks, may spend 50% more time on those tasks than if they just concentrate on one task before starting the other (Richtel, 2003).

ANNOTATING AND HIGHLIGHTING

People like to annotate when they read, especially for in-depth reading. Olsen's study (1994) finds that 63% of the interviewees like annotating or underlining articles. A study by King Research Inc. also reveals that 33% of people photocopy their personal subscriptions and 56% photocopy library collections in order to annotate and/or highlight printed documents (Griffiths and King, 1993). Annotating and highlighting while reading is a common activity in the print environment. Has this "traditional" pattern migrated to the digital environment when we read electronic documents? The answer is no, as indicated by the following survey results.

Table 5.3 shows that nearly 54% of the participants "always" or "frequently" annotate printed documents, compared to approximately 11% "always" or "frequently" annotate electronic documents. It is also interesting to note that over 51% of the respondents report they never annotate electronic documents. However, none of them report never annotating printed documents. Among 113 participants in this survey, only three individuals report they annotate digital documents more frequently than paper documents. In contrast, eighty-five respondents report that they annotate paper

Table 5.3
A Comparison of Annotating Printed and Electronic Documents

Frequency	Printed documents	Electronic documents
Always	21.2%	2.7%
Frequently	32.7%	8.0%
Occasionally	46.0%	38.0%
Never	0%	51.3%
Total	99.9%	100.0%

documents more frequently than electronic documents. Similar findings have been reported in a recent study of e-book use. In a study of e-book use by undergraduate students at Simmons College in the spring of 2006, Hernon and others (2007) find that while it is possible to annotate e-books, only two students do so. Most of them still prefer papercopy over reading on-line because of the convenience of marking up with a pencil or marker. It is interesting to note that some students report that the current system of note-taking works well for them, and they don't see a reason to change even if they could highlight and annotate e-books the same way they do printed works. The pattern of highlighting printed documents versus electronic documents is quite similar to annotating, as indicated by Table 5.4.

Why are people less likely to annotate or highlight digital documents? It seems that many people search or browse digital documents, but when they need to have in-depth reading of some documents, they will print out and then annotate printed documents. This argument is further confirmed by the results presented in Tables 5.5 and 5.6, as well as Table 6.7 (see Chapter 6) about circumstances affecting the choice of reading media by students in China. Annotating electronic documents is certainly possible, but it does re-quire many more resources and additional skills rather than a simple pencil or highlighter (McKnight, 1997). It is still easier to navigate on paper compared to navigating in digital documents. One respondent reports: "I always anno-tate in both languages: my native language and English. I could not find an electronic annotation system that could effectively accommodate my unique

Table 5.4
A Comparison of Highlighting Printed and Electronic Documents

Frequency	Printed documents	Electronic documents
Always	27.4%	2.7%
Frequently	34.5%	5.3%
Occasionally	38.1%	32.7%
Never	0%	59.3%
Total	100.0%	100.0%

situation as paper does. Paper is a versatile medium." As a non-native English speaker, I share a similar experience. In addition to annotating in English, I annotate in Chinese, particularly on some private and sensitive issues.

Another student indicates: "I ran out of ink and I could not print out a class reading from the Web, so I had to read on a computer screen. I just feel as if I missed something because I was not able to use a pen to annotate." These comments further illustrate the importance of direct pen-based interaction when annotating. Marshall (2005) notes: "If we want people to read on the screen, we're going to have to provide them with the facilities to annotate. The standard keyboard–mouse interaction paradigm is not sufficient support for the kind of unselfconscious interaction that we observe in practice."

One respondent reports that "highlighting and annotating digital documents does not come naturally and takes practice." O'Hara and Sellen (1997) also find that annotation on paper is smoothly integrated with reading, but online annotation is distracting.

PRINTING FOR READING

A number of studies have concluded that while the computer has served us well in terms of locating information, it has yet to provide a comparable tool for actually reading that information (Levy, 1997; Sellen and Harper, 1997; 2002). Displays are now much easier to read, although they still suffer in readability when compared to paper. Sathe, Grady, and Giuse (2002) report that the ability to search electronic journals was cited as an advantage, whereas many people still favor the readability of printed journals. Even though e-books are highly portable, issues such as readability, screen size, and slow page turning still persist (Buzzetto-More, Sweat-Guy and Elobaid, 2007).

According to Table 5.5, over 80% of the participants report that they "always" or "frequently" print out electronic documents for reading. But none of the participants report they "never" print out electronic documents for reading. Table 5.6 further shows that nearly 90% of the participants prefer paper as a reading medium to digital media.[4] Only approximately 3% of the participants favor electronic over print media for reading. Commonly cited reasons for the preference for reading on paper include the following:

- "I have spent more time on electronic media than before. However, I still keep the old-fashioned way of reading serious papers through printed media. Electronic readings are just for fun or browsing popular information."
- "Preference of type of document media depends on the kind of reading. I rarely print e-mails anymore, but I prefer printed books to e-books."
- "I really enjoy relaxing when I read. I like it quiet and no distraction when reading for leisure or school-related assignments."

Table 5.5
Frequency of Printing Electronic
Documents for Reading

Frequency	Percentage
Always	10.6%
Frequently	71.7%
Occasionally	17.7%
Never	0%
Total	100.0%

- "For a short article or quick check for news, the screen is fine. But if a document is more than three screens' worth, I will most likely print it out to read."
- "I print out *many* electronic articles. I like the flexibility of paper and comfort reading them."
- "I dislike reading on a screen, especially in-depth."
- "One advantage paper has over its digital counterpart is that it forces finality. Printing on paper provides a sense of permanence of the finished document."

Similar findings have been reported in many other studies. An OCLC (Online Computer Library Center) white paper on the information habits of college students (2002) indicates that students repeatedly mention their needs for printing out electronic documents. Even though people spend numerous hours in front of computer screens, they still don't want to read at length on computers. They tend to print out when faced with more than three or four pages (Rogers, 2006). A recent study of students' perceptions of e-books at the University of Maryland Eastern Shore shows that a majority of the participants usually print out when they need to read a long document online and nearly 55% prefer hardcopy over a digital format (Buzzetto-More, Sweat-Guy and Elobaid, 2007). Survey results in Chapter 9 further reveal that even though the use of electronic sources and online reading habits vary by discipline, the frequency of printing out electronic documents is surprisingly similar across all disciplines.

From the very beginning, readers demanded books in formats adapted to their intended use. Of all the shapes that books have acquired through

Table 5.6
Types of Document Media Prefer to Read

Document media	Percentage
Electronic media	2.7%
Print media	89.4%
Either one is fine	8.0%
Total	100.1%

the ages, the most popular have been those that allowed the book to be held comfortably in the reader's hand. For example, the early Mesopotamian tablets were usually square but sometimes oblong pads of clay, approximately three inches across, and could be held comfortably in the hand (Manguel, 1996). The tradition of holding a book in the hand while reading can partially explain why those views of replacing printed documents with electronic media are overly optimistic. Strassmann (1985) also stresses that the human nervous system has a special control mechanism for the coordination of the hand with the focusing muscles of the eye. It is much easier to read something that is held in the hand than something that just lies on a table. One respondent points out: "I like the flexibility of paper. I simply don't like staring into monitor that is arm-length away for a few hours."

Preference for reading media is related to reading purposes and activities. For example, paper is preferred for situations where the document is long, and when the reader has to fully comprehend the important material, or needs cross-referencing or constant moving (see Table 6.7). When people need to compare and synthesize different documents, they tend to spread out multiple documents. This suggests the need for printing, since the computer screen cannot display conveniently many documents at the same time. Marchionini (2000) reports that students may prefer reading ancient Greek texts on the screen over reading on paper because of the ease in dictionary lookup. Translating words to another language is a function that paper documents do not support. One respondent notes: "It is really convenient to read online. When my cursor points to a specific word that I don't understand, the software offers me the translation."

CONCLUSION

In an increasingly digital environment, readers (especially younger ones) are likely to gradually develop the screen-based reading behavior, and to increasingly use a variety of strategies (e.g., browsing and keyword spotting) to cope with the information-abundant environment. On the other hand, readers will continue to use print media for much of their reading activities, especially in-depth reading. In-depth reading usually involves annotating and highlighting. People's preference for paper as a medium of reading (especially in-depth reading) also implies that paper is unlikely to disappear in the digital age. In the digital age, printing for reading remains one of the major driving forces for the increasing consumption of paper (Liu and Stork, 2000; Sellen and Harper, 2002). A number of digital reading devices have been designed to support reading electronic documents efficiently. Future research efforts can be placed on increasing sustained attention of reading in the digital environment.

Digital technology allows us to have instant access to volumes of information that help us improve comprehension. On the other hand, the improved access creates a new challenge for readers as to what material they choose to read. In a world where choices and opportunities are part of our daily lives, we need to set priorities on the kind of materials we want to access.

Rather than deprecating digital technology as hurting our reading quality in the online environment, we should embrace its potential and expect technological advances will reduce the problems even further. While many people don't see digital libraries as a place for "concentrated reading" but as a highway to access information, we should keep in mind that technology is constantly improving and reading practices themselves are evolving. As Marshall (2005) notes: "It is not enough to simply echo paper's capabilities; in some situations and for some activities, paper is too malleable and too useful to replace. On the other hand, it is possible to create a compelling on-screen reading experience that takes advantage of maturing computer technology to go beyond paper."

This chapter attempts to investigate how people's reading behavior has changed over the past decade by self-reported measures of their overall reading experience. It targets people who are between 30–45 years of age. The inherent limitations of self-reported measures and small sample size of this study mean that the results cannot be generalized across different age groups. Since an entire generation that has grown up with new technology is likely to have different expectations and behaviors toward the use of digital media, studies on the demographic variables are needed to fully validate the findings. Future studies are also needed to explore changes in reading habits in relation to learning.

Most data in this chapter are taken from the U.S. experience. It is generally believed that global reverberations from the impact of digital media on reading will be felt in the United States first. However, it is difficult to know what is unique about the American experience when analyzing the impact of digital media on reading behavior in other cultures. Nevertheless, an analysis of relevant indicators would provide a sensitive yardstick for anticipating reading behavior in the digital environment. Future research can also extend the findings in this chapter by investigating similar research problems in different cultural contexts.

The following chapter will examine in depth gender differences in the online reading environment by analyzing reading behaviors of respondents in another different culture. Circumstances affecting the choice between paper and digital media are also presented.

NOTES

1. Reading in the digital environment has been extensively discussed. For comprehensive reviews of literature related to reading, please see Dillon (1992), Radway (1994), and Ross (2003).

2. Design of the questionnaires: Since this study is dependent on participants having an accurate recollection of their overall reading habits over the past ten years,

careful attention was paid to the adequacy of long-term memories in the design of survey questions and answering scales. It seems unrealistic to ask people to report *detailed* changes; however, it is feasible to ask people to report *general* changes (e.g., increasing, decreasing, no change). If participants don't remember, they can select the "don't know" category. A pilot study of over twenty individuals was conducted in the spring of 2003 to pretest the survey questions. The pilot study also confirms the above assumption. Final questions of this study were developed based on the pilot study as well as on other related studies. The response categories for questions 1–5 include "more time," "less time," "no change," and "don't know;" for questions 6–11 include "increasing," "decreasing," "no change," and "don't know;" for questions 12–16 include "always," "frequently," "occasionally," and "never;" and for question 17 include "electronic media," "printed media," and "either one is fine."

3. How was the survey conducted? The amount of time spent on reading varies widely among different age groups. This study focuses on people who are between 30–45 years old. Since the purpose of this study is to explore the impact of digital media on reading behavior, people who have extensive experience in reading digital documents were selected. Two hundred and fifty copies of questionnaires were distributed in the summer and fall of 2003: 160 copies were distributed by mail to engineers, scientists, accountants, teachers, and managers in various organizations, and 90 copies were distributed to graduate students at San Jose State University in class. Therefore, this is a sample of convenience rather than a random sample. Participants were informed that the purpose of this study is to explore the impact of digital media on reading behavior. They were asked to fill out the questionnaires based on their own experiences with reading. Among 119 returned copies, 113 are complete and 6 are incomplete. Results of those 113 complete questionnaires are presented in Tables 5.1–5.6.

4. When it comes to readability, digital media cannot compete with print even in the advent of electronic paper. Electronic paper was developed in order to overcome some of the limitations of computer monitors. It offers unique properties, such as flexibility, brightness, minimal power requirements, and ultra-thinness. Although the readability of e-paper is recognized to be better than that of a conventional display, there is still a gap in readability compared to traditional paper. Please see http://www.imaging.org/store/epub.cfm?abstrid=31886.

REFERENCES

Adler, A., Gujar, A., Harrison, B., O'Hara, K., and Sellen, A.J. (1998). A Diary Study of Work-Related Reading: Design Implication for Digital Reading Devices. In *Proceeding of CHI'98 Conference* (pp. 241–248). New York, NY: ACM Press.

Almind, T.C. and Ingwersen, P. (1997). Informatric Analyses on the World Wide Web: Methodological Approaches to "Webometrics." *Journal of Documentation*, 53(4), 404–426.

AlShaali, S. and Varshney, U. (2005). On the Usability of Mobile Commerce. *International Journal of Mobile Communications*, 3(1), 29–37.

Berkenkotter, C. and Huckin, T.N. (1993). Rethinking Genre from a Sociocognitive Perspective. *Written Communication*, 10(4), 475–509.

Birkerts, S. (1994). The *Gutenberg Elegies: The Fate of Reading in an Electronic Age*. Boston, MA: Faber and Faber.

Birkerts, S. (1996). Reading in the Electronic Era. *Logos*, 7(3), 211–214.

Bolter, J.D. (1991). *Writing Spaces: The Computer, Hypertext, and the History of Writing*. Hillsdale, NJ: L. Erlbaum Associates.

Buzzetto-More, N., Sweat-Guy, R. and Elobaid, M. (2007). Reading in a Digital Age: e-Books Are Students Ready for This Learning Object? *Interdisciplinary Journal of Knowledge and Learning Objects*, 3, 239–250.

Darnton, R. (1989). Towards a History of Reading. *Wilson Quarterly*, 13(4), 87–102.

Dillon, A. (1992). Reading from Paper versus Screens: A Critical Review of the Empirical Literature. *Ergonomics*, 35(10), 1297–1326.

Eveland, W.P. and Dunwoody, S. (2001). User Control and Structural Isomorphism or Disorientation and Cognitive Load? Learning from the Web versus Print. *Communication Research*, 28(1), 48–78.

Goldsborough, R. (2000). Text Demands Respect on the Web. *Advertising Age*, 71(32), 44.

Gordon, M.D. (1997). It's 10 A.M. Do You Know Where Your Documents Are? The Nature and Scope of Information Retrieval Problem in Business. *Information Processing and Management*, 33(1), 107–121.

Griffiths, J. and King, D.W. (1993). *Special Libraries: Increasing the Information Edge*. Washington, DC: Special Library Association.

Hartzell, G. (2002). Paper Lion. *School Library Journal*, 48(9), 37.

Healy, J.M. (1990). *Endangered Minds: Why Our Children Don't Think*. New York, NY: Simon and Schuster.

Hernon, P., Hopprt, R., Leach, M.R., Saunders, L.L., and Zhang, J. (2007). E-book Use by Students: Undergraduates in Economics, Literature, and Nursing. *Journal of Academic Librarianship*, 33(1), 3–13.

Knulst, W.P., Kraaykamp, G., van den Broek, A., and de Haan, J. (1996). Reading Habits: 50 Years of Research on Reading and Threats to Reading: Cultural Foundations. Retrieved October 28, 2003, from http://www.scp.nl/boeken/studies/studie23/uk/samenvatting.htm.

Landow, G.P. (1992). *Hypertext: The Convergence of Technology and Contemporary Critical Theory*. Baltimore, MD: Johns Hopkins University Press.

Lanham, R.A. (1993). *The Electronic Word: Technology, Democracy, and the Arts*. Chicago, IL: University of Chicago Press.

Lanham, R.A. (1995). Digital Literacy. *Scientific American*, 273(3), 198–200.

Levy, D.M. (1997). I Read the News Today, Oh Boy: Reading and Attention in Digital Libraries. In *Proceedings of the 2nd ACM International Conference on Digital Libraries* (pp. 202–211). New York, NY: ACM Press.

Liu, Z. and Stork, D. (2000). Is Paperless Really More? Rethinking the Role of Paper in the Digital Age. *Communications of the ACM*, 43(11), 94–97.

Manguel, A. (1996). *A History of Reading*. New York, NY: Viking.

Marchionini, G. (2000). Evaluating Digital Libraries: A Longitudinal and Multi-faceted View. *Library Trends*, 49(2), 304–333.

Marshall, C.C. (2005). Reading and Interactivity in the Digital Library: Creating an Experience that Transcends Paper. In D. Marcum and G. George (Eds.), *Digital Library Development: The View from Kanazawa* (pp. 127–145).

Westport, CT: Libraries Unlimited. Retrieved February 23, 2008, from http://www.csdl.tamu.edu/~marshall/KIT-CLIR-revised.pdf.

McKnight, C. (1997). Electronic Journals: What do Users Think of Them? In *Proceedings of International Symposium on Research, Development and Practice in Digital Libraries*. Tsukuba, Japan. Retrieved June 23, 2008, from http://www.dl.slis.tsukuba.ac.jp/ISDL97/proceedings/mcknight.html.

Miall, D.S. and Dobson, T. (2001). Reading Hypertext and the Experience of Literature. *Journal of Digital Information*, 2(1). Retrieved February 23, 2008, from http://jodi.ecs.soton.ac.uk/Articles/v02/i01/Miall/.

Michie, D. (1996). Scan, Annotate and Pass on.... *New Scientist*, 149(2013), 48–49.

Murphy, P.K., Long, J.F., Holleran, T.A., and Esterly, E. (2003). Persuasion Online or on Paper: A New Take on an Old Issue. *Learning and Instruction*, 13(5), 511–532.

Murray, J.H. (1997). *Hamlet on the Holodeck: The Future of Narrative in Cyberspace*. Boston, MA: MIT Press.

Nunberg, G. (1993). The Places of Books in the Age of Electronic Reproduction. In R.H. Bloch and C. Hesse (Eds.), *Future Libraries* (pp. 13–37). Berkeley, CA: University of California Press.

OCLC White Paper on the Information Habits of College Students (2002). How Academic Librarians Can Influence Students' Web-Based Information Choices. Retrieved February 23, 2008, from http://www5.oclc.org/downloads/community/informationhabits.pdf.

O'Hara, K. and Sellen, A. (1997). A Comparison of Reading Paper and Online Documents. In *Proceedings of CHI'97 Conference* (pp. 335–342). New York, NY: ACM Press.

Olsen, J. (1994). *Electronic Journal Literature: Implications for Scholars*. London, England: Mecklermedia.

Poynter Institute. (2000). Eye-Tracking Study Conducted by the Poynter Institute and Stanford University. Retrieved February 1, 2007, from http://www.poynter.org/eyetrack2000/.

Radway, J. (1994). Beyond Mary Bailey and Old Maid Librarians: Reimagining Readers and Rethinking Reading. *Journal of Education for Library and Information Science*, 35(4), 275–296.

Ramirez, E. (2003). The Impact of the Internet on the Reading Practices of a University Community: The Case of UNAM. In *Proceedings of the 69th IFLA General Conference and Council*. Retrieved October 23, 2007, from http://www.ifla.org/IV/ifla69/papers/019e-Ramirez.pdf.

Richtel, M. (2003, July 7). Wired to an Addiction: Multitaskers Get and Need the Rush. *International Herald Tribune*. Retrieved March 7, 2004, from http://www.iht.com/articles/101895.html.

Rogers, M. (2006). Ebooks Struggling to Find a Niche. *Library Journal*, 131(11), 25–26.

Ross, C.S. (2003). Reading in a Digital Age. Retrieved February 23, 2008, from http://www.camls.org/ce/ross.pdf.

Sathe, N.A., Grady, J.L., and Giuse, N.B. (2002). Print versus Electronic Journals: A Preliminary Investigation into the Effect of Journal Format on Research Processes. *Journal of the Medical Library Association*, 90(2), 235–243.

Sellen, A. and Harper, R. (1997). Paper as an Analytic Resource for the Design of New Technologies. In *Proceedings of CHI'97 Conference* (pp. 319–326). New York, NY: ACM Press.

Sellen, A. and Harper, R. (2002). *The Myth of the Paperless Office.* Cambridge, MA: MIT Press.

Stoll, C. (1995). *Silicon Snake Oil: Second Thoughts on the Information Highway.* New York, NY: Doubleday.

Strassmann, P.A. (1985). *Information Payoff.* New York, NY: The Free Press.

Thirunarayanan, M. (2003). From Thinkers to Clickers: The World Wide Web and the Transformation of the Essence of Being Human. *Ubiquity,* 4(12). Retrieved February 23, 2008, from http://www.acm.org/ubiquity/views/m_thirunarayanan_8.html.

Topping, K.J. (1997). Electronic Literacy in School and Home: A Look into the Future. International Reading Association, Inc. Retrieved February 23, 2008, from http://www.readingonline.org/international/future/.

6

---•••---

GENDER DIFFERENCES IN THE ONLINE READING ENVIRONMENT

We live in an online environment. Technological advances have made e-books and digital libraries a reality. Although many readers still don't like reading on glowing computer screens and continue to print out for reading, digital technologies have already begun to affect reading practice and behavior as people spend more time reading online.

Gender differences in Web information seeking have attracted considerable interest (Hupfer and Deltor, 2006; Schumacher and Morahan-Martin, 2001; Smith and Whitlark, 2001; Weiser, 2000). However, little attention has been given to the study of gender differences in online reading behavior. This chapter will examine gender differences in online reading: to what extent do male and female readers differ in the preference for reading media and in the overall satisfaction with online reading? Does gender play a role in handling digital documents and in the changes of reading behavior? Understanding these issues would enable us to serve the needs of readers more responsively and to empower readers in the online environment.

GENDER DIFFERENCES IN ONLINE READING

Gender has been identified as a strong demographic factor that influences information behavior (Taylor, 1991; Wilson, 1999). Gender has also been

This chapter is an updated and expanded version of an earlier article: Liu, Z. and Huang, X. (2008). Gender differences in the Online Reading Environment. *Journal of Documentation*, 64(4), 616–626.

Table 6.1
Gender Differences in the Preference for Reading Media

Document media	Male (n = 80)	Female (n = 123)
Electronic media	12.5%	5.7%
Print media	51.3%	73.2%
Either one is fine	36.3%	21.1%

Note: Figures of this and other tables may not add to 100% because of rounding.

identified as a strong predictor of attitudes and behavior in Web information seeking. In a recent article, Hupfer and Detlor (2006) note that certain male–female differences in Web searching appear to persist. For example, women tend to use the Web to e-mail, chat, and search reference materials about medical and government information. Men, however, tend to focus on information about investment, purchase, and personal interests. Wolin and Korgaonkar (2003) find that males are more likely than females to surf the Web for functional and entertainment purposes, whereas females are more likely to surf the Web for shopping reasons. In a recent study, Karim and Hasan (2007) analyze the reading habits and attitudes of 127 undergraduate students in Malaysia. They find that a Web site is seen as an increasingly important reading source. Their result also indicates that gender is significantly associated with reading certain types of reading materials (e.g., newspapers, literature, and Web sites). Male students read significantly more newspapers, more Web sites, and more literature than female students. However, Ross (2002) reports that females tend to read more than males.

Table 6.1 shows that male and female readers differ in medium preference. Female readers have a stronger preference for paper as a reading medium than male readers: 73.2% of female readers prefer print media compared to 51.3% of males, and only 5.7% of females favor digital media compared to 12.5% of males ($x^2 = 10.379, p < 0.01$).

On the other hand, males' and females' ratings of their overall online experience are different. As indicated by Table 6.2, female readers in this survey tend to have a greater degree of dissatisfaction with online reading than males. Only 22.0% of female readers have a positive experience with online reading compared to 30.0% of male readers, and 30.9% of females dislike

Table 6.2
Gender Differences in Online Reading Experience

Document media	Male (n = 80)	Female (n = 123)
Positive	30.0%	22.0%
Negative	18.8%	30.9%

Table 6.3
Gender Differences in Handling Electronic Documents

Frequency	Print Out		Download		Bookmark	
	Male	Female	Male	Female	Male	Female
Always	8.8	11.4	16.3	23.6	6.3	4.9
Frequently	25.0	26.0	52.5	46.3	22.5	15.4
Occasionally	53.8	56.9	30.0	29.3	43.8	45.5
Never	12.5	5.7	1.3	0.8	27.5	34.1

Note: Male: n = 80, Female: n = 123. Figures given are percentages.

online reading in contrast to only 18.8% of male readers ($x^2 = 3.90$, $p < 0.05$).

Table 6.3 shows gender differences in handling electronic documents when they read online. Survey results reveal that female readers tend to print out electronic documents for reading more frequently than males, whereas male readers tend to bookmark electronic documents for future reading more often than females. 37.4% of female readers report that they "always" or "frequently" print out electronic documents for reading, compared to 33.8% of males. However, 28.8% of male readers "always" or "frequently" bookmark Web documents, in contrast to 20.3% of female readers. But these differences are not statistically significant. Similar findings are reported in a study of Web searching behavior of sixth-grade students. Large, Beheshti, and Rahman (2002) find that groups of boys on the average save more images than girls.

With the growing amount of digital information available and the increasing amount of time people spend on reading electronic media, the digital environment has already begun to affect people's reading behavior. Based on a survey of 113 people who have extensive experience in online reading in the United States, Chapter 5 indicates that a screen-based reading behavior is emerging. The screen-based reading behavior is characterized by more time on browsing and scanning, one-time reading, nonlinear reading, and reading more selectively, while less time is spent on in-depth reading, concentrated reading, and decreasing sustained attention. As shown in Table 6.4, overall online reading behavior of Chinese readers is quite similar to that of American readers.

According to Table 6.4, a higher percentage of male readers in this survey report increasing time spent on browsing and scanning (71.3% vs. 66.7%), one-time reading (52.5% vs. 39.8%), and nonlinear reading such as jumps (77.5% vs. 69.1%) than female readers. This suggests that male readers tend to be more interactively engaged in the online reading environment than female readers. Similar findings are reported in a study of Web-searching

Table 6.4
Gender Differences in the Changes in Reading Behavior

Percentage of time spent on	Increasing		Decreasing		No change		Don't know		Significant
	Male	Female	Male	Female	Male	Female	Male	Female	
Browsing and scanning	71.3	66.7	13.8	22.0	6.3	6.5	8.8	4.9	
In-depth reading	28.8	27.6	57.5	50.4	8.8	16.2	5.0	5.7	
Concentrated reading	36.3	42.3	45.0	36.6	12.5	16.2	6.3	4.9	
One-time reading	52.5	39.8	36.3	42.3	8.8	12.2	2.5	5.7	
Reading selectively	85.0	64.2	6.3	21.1	7.5	11.4	1.3	3.2	*
Nonlinear reading	77.5	69.1	10.0	13.0	11.3	11.4	1.3	6.5	
Sustained attention	26.3	13.0	57.5	74.0	12.5	8.9	3.8	4.1	*

Note: Male: n = 80, Female: n = 123. Figures given are percentages.

behavior of sixth-grade students by Large, Beheshti, and Rahman (2002). They find that boys click more hyperlinks per minute than girls, and boys tend to perform more page jumps per minute than girls. Not surprisingly, a higher proportion of male readers report lower in-depth reading (57.5% vs. 50.4%) and decreasing concentrated reading (45.0% vs. 36.6%) than female readers. However, these differences do not reach statistical significance.

In the online environment, readers need to cope with a massive amount of text and read selectively. In addition to coping with potentially distracting colorful or blinking graphics, audio, and video, readers often become disoriented because they have to make constant choices on which hyperlink to click or whether to scroll further down, rather than devoting full attention to reading (Charney, 1994; Schmar-Dobler, 2003; Thirunarayanan, 2003). Hupfer and Deltor (2006) also note that men naturally tend to be more selective in Web searching. Women, however, tend to make a greater effort and employ a more conscientious approach. Table 6.4 reveals that there are two significant differences between male and female readers on the dimension of reading selectively and sustained attention. Compared to 64.2% of female readers, 85.0% of male readers report that they read things more selectively ($x^2 = 10.6$, $p < 0.01$). On the other hand, a higher percentage of female readers report decreasing sustained attention in the online environment than male readers (74.0% vs. 57.5%; $x^2 = 6.61$, $p < 0.025$). These two differences are statistically significant. Ford and Miller (1996) find similar gender differences in the Internet searching: Men tend to enjoy browsing, while women seem disoriented by the Internet.

WHY MALE READERS AND FEMALE READERS DIFFER IN THE ONLINE READING ENVIRONMENT?

Explanations for why male readers and female readers differ in the preference for reading media and in the overall satisfaction with online reading include the following:

First, *female readers demonstrate stronger preference for as well as greater reliance on paper as a reading medium than male readers.* This is one of the major reasons why female readers are less happy with online reading than males. As Table 6.5 and Figure 6.1 indicate, there is a significant relationship between online reading satisfaction and reading medium preference. The extent of online reading satisfaction is positively related to the degree of preference for electronic media. For example, 1.9% who have a negative online reading experience, 5.1% who have a neutral experience, 20.5% who have a satisfactory experience, and 28.6% who have a enjoyable experience, prefer electronic media. Meanwhile, it is not surprising to find that the extent of online reading satisfaction is negatively related to the degree of preference for printed media. In other words, the higher the dissatisfaction with online reading, the

Table 6.5
Cross-Tabulation: Online Reading Experience and Medium Preference

Experience with online reading	Prefer electronic media	Prefer print media	Either one is fine	Total
Enjoyable	2 (28.6%)	2 (28.6%)	3 (42.9%)	7 (100.1%)
Satisfactory	9 (20.5%)	19 (43.2%)	16 (36.4%)	44 (100.1%)
Neutral	5 (5.1%)	62 (62.6%)	32 (32.3%)	99 (100.0%)
Not comfortable	1 (1.9%)	48 (90.6%)	4 (7.5%)	53 (100.0%)
Total	17 (8.4%)	131 (64.5%)	55 (27.1%)	203 (100.0%)

Note: Male: n = 80, Female: n = 123.

stronger the preference for print media. For example, 90.6% who have a negative online reading experience, 62.6% who have a neutral experience, 43.2% who have a satisfactory experience, and 28.6% who have a enjoyable experience, prefer paper as a reading medium. This finding is consistent with the results presented in Tables 6.1 and 6.2.

Second, *female readers are more linear and thorough readers*. In the print environment, female readers tend to annotate more often than male readers, which clearly indicates that females are likely more serious readers than males. The dramatic shift to an online reading environment may present a challenge and frustration to this habit, since digital documents are not as convenient to annotate as paper documents. This is another factor contributing to the

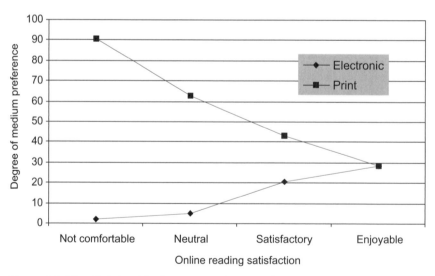

Figure 6.1 The Relationship between Online Reading Satisfaction and Medium Preference.

Table 6.6
Annotating Printed and Electronic Documents (Males versus Females)

Frequency	Printed documents		Electronic documents	
	Male	Female	Male	Female
Always	16.3	27.6	2.5	1.6
Frequently	27.5	26.0	6.3	4.9
Occasionally	46.3	38.2	47.5	41.5
Never	10.0	8.1	43.8	52.0

Note: Male: n = 80, Female: n = 123. Figures given are percentages.

differences in the preference for reading media and in the overall satisfaction with online reading. Table 6.6 shows that 53.6% of female readers "always" or "frequently" annotate printed documents while reading, compared to 43.8% of male readers. But in the online environment, female readers tend to annotate not as frequently as male readers. Compared to 43.8% of male readers, 52.0% of female readers never annotate electronic documents. This argument is further supported by their practice in handing electronic documents: female readers tend to print out electronic documents for reading more frequently than males (see Table 6.3). Large, Beheshti, and Rahman (2002) find that girls spend more time reading individual pages on the Web than boys. This implies that female readers are likely to read things more seriously than male readers. Ray and Chi (2003) report that girls have a tendency to browse entire linked documents and are more linear and thorough navigators than boys.

Third, *males are more active browsers.* Digital media introduce a number of attractive advantages that are absent in the traditional print environment, such as interactivity, nonlinearity, immediacy of accessing information, and the convergence of text, images, audio, and video (Landow, 1992; Lanham, 1993; Murray, 1997; Ross, 2003). Digital media are ideal for browsing or casual reading instead of in-depth or serious reading (see Table 6.7). Large, Beheshti, and Rahman (2002) find that boys' groups are more actively engaged in browsing than girls' groups. Perhaps, this is another reason why male readers have a greater satisfaction than female readers. A number of studies also suggest boys, in general, are more experienced users on the Web and have more positive attitudes toward technology (Leong and Hawamdeh, 1999; Ray and Chi, 2003; Schumacher and Morahan-Martin, 2001).

CONCLUSION

This chapter demonstrates that there are some significant differences between male and female readers in the online reading environment. Understanding these issues would enable us to better understand the changing

Table 6.7
Ten Most Frequently Cited Circumstances Affecting the Choice of Reading Media

Prefer reading online over reading on paper	Prefer reading on paper over reading online
When I read short documents.	When I read lengthy documents (e.g., novels, textbooks).
When I do casual reading (e.g., news and entertainment).	When I need serious/in-depth reading.
When the document is easy to understand.	When I read something that is difficult to understand.
When I need the most recent information.	When I read scholarly/research papers.
When I need information at the last minute (e.g., easy to copy and paste).	When I read something that is very important and interesting (e.g., preservation).
When I need browsing (e.g., not sure the document is exactly what I need).	When I need to take notes (e.g., annotation).
When I want one-time reading only.	When I need multiple-time reading.
When music is embedded in the document.	When I need cross-referencing.
When I want to save money (e.g., cost in printing documents).	When I need constant moving (e.g., portability).
When I feel bored.	When I feel calm and relaxed.

reading behavior in the online environment, and to develop more effective digital reading devices.

People spend an increasing amount of time reading online. Yet, the practices of online reading in networked environments are not well understood. This chapter extends Chapter 5 in several ways. In Chapter 5, we investigated how people's reading behavior has changed by targeting people living in the United States who are 30–45 years old. However, it is difficult to know what is unique about the American experience when understanding the impact of digital media on reading behavior in other cultures. By examining similar issues in a different age group (18–23 years old) and in another different culture, we are able to have a cross-cultural perspective of reading in the online environment.[1,2]

Comparisons with Previous Studies

In a study of reading practices of students at the National University of Mexico, Ramirez (2003) finds that approximately 78% of college students prefer to read in print and 18% favor reading on screen. In a study of 113

Table 6.8
Preference for Reading Media: American Readers versus Chinese Readers

Document media	American readers (n = 113)*	Chinese readers (n = 203)
Electronic media	2.7%	8.4%
Print media	89.4%	64.5%
Either one is fine	8.0%	27.1%

Note: *Data derived from Chapter 5.

American readers who are between 30 and 45 years of age, Chapter 5 shows that nearly 90% of the participants prefer paper as a reading medium and 3% favor digital media for reading purposes. As indicated in Table 6.8, Chinese readers also prefer paper as a reading medium over digital media, even though their preference for paper is not as overwhelming as American readers. Nearly 65% of Chinese readers in this survey cite paper as their favorite reading medium, and over 27% of Chinese readers express no preference compared to only 8% of American readers ($x^2 = 22.97, p < 0.001$). Table 6.8 indicates that American and Chinese readers differ significantly in medium preference. The stronger reliance on paper as a reading medium by American readers is further supported by the difference in printing frequency. American readers print out electronic documents for reading much more frequently than Chinese online readers ($x^2 = 70.93, p < 0.001$). Differences in the findings from this study with the previous research could be attributed to differences in the populations being examined. This chapter analyzes online reading behavior of undergraduate students and graduate students in China (18–23 years old) as opposed to the examination of online reading behavior of people who are 30–45 years old in the United States (see Chapter 5). Generational difference is perhaps an important factor contributing to the difference in the extent of preference. It seems that an entire generation that is growing up with new technology is likely to have different expectations and experiences toward the use of digital media. It is also possible that these differences are caused by cultural differences. Future studies on generational differences and cultural differences are needed to fully validate this finding.

The Future of Print Media

Despite a different extent in the preference among different genders and cultures (e.g., American, Chinese, and Mexican), we find that the preference for reading printed text remains strong. This clearly indicates that paper is unlikely to disappear in the digital age, because reading print media is deeply embedded in tradition. According to Table 6.5, it is not surprising to find that 90.6% of the respondents who rate online reading "not comfortable" prefer paper as a reading medium. However, it is very interesting to note that

62.6% who have a neutral experience with online reading prefer print media, and only 20.5% among those who have satisfactory online reading experience favor electronic media. Findings in Chapter 5 reveal that annotating while reading is a common activity in the print environment. However, this "traditional" pattern has not yet migrated to the digital environment when people read electronic documents. This argument is further confirmed in the survey of young Chinese online readers: only 7.4% of the respondents report that they "always" or "frequently" annotate electronic documents. In contrast, 48.8% never annotate any electronic documents while reading. When it comes to readability, digital media cannot compete with print. As shown in Table 6.7, the need for reading lengthy documents, the need for serious/in-depth reading, and the need for note taking are among the most frequently cited circumstances that people prefer reading on paper over reading online.

Digital media and print media have their unique advantages and limitations. Each plays a different role and serves the needs of users in different circumstances (see Table 6.7). In the digital age, printing for serious reading and annotating remains one of the major driving forces for the increasing consumption of paper (Liu and Stork, 2000; Sellen and Harper, 2002).

The arrival of digital media brings both positive and negative possibilities. Even though in the future people are likely to read more from a screen than from a printed page, we must also keep in mind that readers' purposes and preferences are very diverse due to differences in gender and age, and that there is not a single format that is ideal to all. It is unlikely that digital media will render traditional books and libraries obsolete in the foreseeable future (see Chapters 9–10 for more discussion).

Limitations and Future Studies

This chapter attempts to explore gender differences in the online reading environment by targeting undergraduate and graduate students in a major university in China. Since all university students in China must take a few required classes, we selected students in required classes as subjects of this study with the goal of achieving a comprehensive coverage of students from diverse disciplines. However, this is a sample of convenience rather than a random sample of students. It is still likely that students in various disciplines are not equally represented. We acknowledge that the generalizability of our results may be affected by our reliance on a convenience sample of students. The inherent limitations of self-reported measures and small sample size of this study mean that the results cannot be generalized across different age groups and cultures. Future research can extend the findings of this study by investigating similar research problems in different age groups and cultural contexts, and reasons for choosing one format over another.

NOTES

1. How was the survey conducted? The World Wide Web (WWW) is becoming a pervasive resource for scholars and students in China. Undergraduate and graduate students were selected as the subjects of this study for two reasons: (1) They are among the heaviest online readers in China; (2) Since undergraduate and graduate students in this study are mostly 18–23-year old students, the impact of generational differences on reading is kept to a minimum. Two hundred and forty copies of the questionnaire were distributed to students at Zhongshan University in Guangzhou (one of the major universities in China) during the spring of 2006. Participants were informed that the purpose of this study is to explore the impact of digital media on reading behavior. They were asked to fill out the questionnaires based on their own experiences with reading. Participants in this study are undergraduate and graduate students from diverse disciplines such as business administration, computer science, economics, engineering, library and information science, mathematics, physics, and sociology. Two hundred three completed copies were returned: 100 copies from graduate students and 103 from undergraduate students. Among 203 respondents in this survey, 80 are males and 123 females.

2. The survey questions in this study are based on that in Chapter 5. Since most undergraduate and graduate students in China possess a good command of English, the questionnaire includes English and Chinese versions with the goal of achieving the greatest degree of consistency and comparability with Chapter 5. As a matter of fact, several students answered the survey questions in English.

REFERENCES

Charney, D. (1994). The Effect of Hypertext on Processes of Reading and Writing. In C. L. Selfe and S. Hilligoss (Eds.), *Literacy and Computers: The Complications of Teaching and Learning with Technology* (pp. 238–263). New York, NY: Modern Language Association.

Ford, N. and Miller, D. (1996). Gender Differences in Internet Perception and Use. In M. Collier and K. Arnold (Eds.), *Electronic Library and Visual Information Research, Papers from the Third ELVIRA Conference* (pp. 87–100). London, England: ASLIB.

Hupfer, M.E. and Detlor, B. (2006). Gender and Web Information Seeking: A Self-Concept Orientation Model. *Journal of the American Society for Information Science and Technology*, 57(8), 1105–1115.

Karim, N. and Hasan, A. (2007). Reading Habits and Attitude in the Digital Age: Analysis of Gender and Academic Program Differences in Malaysia. *The Electronic Libraries*, 25(3), 285–298.

Landow, G.P. (1992). *Hypertext: The Convergence of Technology and Contemporary Critical Theory*. Baltimore, MD: Johns Hopkins University Press.

Lanham, R.A. (1993). *The Electronic Word: Technology, Democracy, and the Arts*. Chicago, IL: University of Chicago Press.

Large, A., Beheshti, J. and Rahman, T. (2002). Gender Differences in Collaborative Web Searching Behavior: An Elementary School Study. *Information Processing and Management*, 38(3), 427–443.

Leong, S. and Hawamdeh, S. (1999). Gender and Learning Attitudes in Using Web-Based Science Lessons. *Information Research*, 5(1). Retrieved November 3, 2006, from http://informationr.net/ir/5-1/paper66.html.

Liu, Z. and Stork, D. (2000). Is Paperless Really More? Rethinking the Role of Paper in the Digital Age. *Communications of the ACM*, 43(11), 94–97.

Murray, J.H. (1997). *Hamlet on the Holodeck: The Future of Narrative in Cyberspace*. Boston, MA: MIT Press.

Ramirez, E. (2003). The Impact of the Internet on the Reading Practices of a University Community: The case of UNAM. *Proceedings of the 69th IFLA General Conference and Council*. Retrieved November 3, 2006, from http://www.ifla.org/IV/ifla69/papers/019e-Ramirez.pdf.

Ray, M. and Chi, M. (2003). Gender Differences in Patterns of Searching the Web. *Journal of Educational Computer Research*, 29(3), 335–348.

Ross, C.S. (2002). Reading in a Digital Age. In G.E. Gorman (Ed.), The *Digital Factor in Library and Information Services* (*International Yearbook of Library and Information Management 2002/2003*) (pp. 91–111). London, England: Facet Publishing.

Ross, C.S. (2003). Reading in a Digital Age. Retrieved February 24, 2008, from http://www.camls.org/ce/ross.pdf.

Schmar-Dobler, E. (2003). Reading on the Internet: The Link Between Literacy and Technology. *Journal of Adolescent and Adult Literacy*, 47(1), 80–85.

Schumacher, P. and Morahan-Martin, J. (2001). Gender, Internet and Computer Attitudes and Experiences. *Computers in Human Behavior*, 17 (1), 95–110.

Sellen, A. and Harper, R. (2002). *The Myth of the Paperless Office*. Cambridge, MA: MIT Press.

Smith, S.M. and Whitlark, D. (2001). Men and Women Online: What Makes Them Click? *Marketing Research*, 13(2), 20–25.

Taylor, R.S. (1991). Information Use Environment. In B. Dervin and M.J. Voigt (Eds.), *Progress in communication sciences* (Vol.10, pp. 217–255). Norward, NJ: Ablex Publishing.

Thirunarayanan, M. (2003). From Thinkers to Clickers: The World Wide Web and the Transformation of the Essence of Being Human. *Ubiquity*, 4(12). Retrieved February 20, 2008, from http://www.acm.org/ubiquity/views/m_thirunarayanan_8.html.

Weiser, E.B. (2000). Gender Differences in Internet Use Patterns and Internet Application Preferences: A Two-Sample Comparison. *CyberPsychology and Behavior*, 3(2), 167–177.

Wilson, T.D. (1999). Models in Information Behaviour Research. *Journal of Documentation*, 55(3), 249–270.

Wolin, L.D. and Korgaonkar, P. (2003). Web Advertising: Gender Differences in Beliefs, Attitudes, and Behavior. *Internet Research*, 13(5), 375–385.

7

PERCEPTIONS OF THE CREDIBILITY
OF SCHOLARLY INFORMATION
ON THE WEB

The advent of the Internet as a new and widely used channel for the delivery of information raises the question of the credibility of information. As the number of documents grows exponentially, selecting documents that are credible and believable demands considerable cognitive efforts. This problem is becoming even more severe under the World Wide Web (WWW), since there is an increasing number of documents coming from self-publishing, which are freed from the traditional refereed mechanism. No one has to review the content of these documents before they are posted on the Web. Because of the relative lack of professional gatekeepers that traditionally serve to validate scholarly publications, scholarly information on the Web usually does not go through the same level of scrutiny (Metzger et al., 2003). Johnson and Kaye (1998) further point out that the lack of refereed process has led to less social and professional pressure to ensure the accuracy of Web-based information. As a result, making judgments of information credibility becomes a new challenge for most users. Priscilla Vail notes that "the educated person used to be the one who could find information; now, with a flood of data available, the educated mind is not the one that can master the facts, but the one able to ask the 'winnowing question'" (cited in Healy, 1990).

With the Web, it matters little where the Web site is located. However, the improved access to documents makes which document to believe and

---

This chapter is an updated and expanded version of an earlier article: Liu, Z. (2004). Perceptions of Credibility of Scholarly Information on the Web. *Information Processing and Management*, 40(6), 1027–1038.

use a much more central concern. This problem has received little attention, perhaps because it is an end users' problem more than a document providers' problem (Buckland and Plaunt, 1997). Previous studies on the credibility of scholarly information on the Web focus on scholars and faculty (Herring, 2001; Rieh, 2002). However, credibility assessment by nonexpert user groups (e.g., graduate and undergraduate students) is still unclear. Only a very small number of studies have specifically examined credibility measurements. Understanding students' credibility assessment is increasingly important as they use Web-based information to do their assignments and conduct research. They are also heavily involved in credibility evaluation.

The goal of this chapter is to approach credibility assessment from a different perspective. Instead of focusing on how scholars judge credibility, this chapter attempts to investigate factors influencing students' perception of the credibility of scholarly information on the Web.

Every study of credibility assessment must first start with the definition of the term "credibility." The dictionary definition of "credible" is "believable, plausible, or worthy of confidence." The root word is from the Latin *credere*, meaning, "to believe" (Hawkins, 1999). Credibility can be simply defined as believability. Credible information is usually referred to as believable information (Fogg et al., 2001). On the other hand, credibility is defined "not as an objective property of the source, but as a receiver perception" (Gunther, 1992). In other words, credibility "is a perceived quality; it doesn't reside in an object, a person, or a piece of information" (Fogg et al., 2001). Credibility does not exist within the information itself, but is rather a characteristic perceived by readers.

People tend to use multiple criteria in their credibility assessment. Credibility is a very complex concept. It is almost inseparable and indeed closely related to trustfulness, reliability, accuracy, authority, and quality (Rieh, 2002). At an operational level, information credibility is referred to as the extent to which users think that information is truthful, unbiased, accurate, reputable, competent, and current.

Scholarly examination of credibility is perhaps among the oldest lines in communication research, originating with the ancient Greeks (Self, 1996). The arrival of the Internet raises this old concept to a new level of importance. Under a large uncontrolled Web environment, we are moving in some settings from relations based on authority ranking to relations based on equality matching (Fiske, 1991). We sacrifice authority for equality and become "hunters and gathers in an information age" (Meyrowitz, 1985).

Differentiating credible information from the deceptive one is not a new problem. However, unraveling in a large uncontrolled Web environment is problematic (Burbules, 2001). The primary value of a document is that it influences a decision, since people always rely on available information for decision-making. However, for the information to have any impact on decision-making, it should first be perceived as credible. Given that credibility strongly influences the impact of a document, it becomes important to understand factors affecting people's decisions on what to believe (Wathen and Burkell, 2002). Credibility criteria used in assessing information have been studied within a wide range of disciplines, notably library and information science, marketing, mass communications, and health sciences.

Most studies in library and information science about document evaluation and selection focus on the relevance of the document. It is not until recently that there appeared a handful of studies on the credibility of information on the Web. Lynch (2001) stresses "the need for information retrieval systems to permit users to factor in trust preferences about this information" and the need to integrate trust and provenance into information retrieval systems. Rieh and Belkin (1998) examine information quality and cognitive authority ratings used by scholars for information on the Web. They identify the following seven factors that users employ to make judgments of quality of information on the Web: source, content, format, presentation, currency, accuracy, and speed of loading. Rieh (2002) reports that scholars perceive the cognitive authority when the information looks "scholarly," and they tend to give high authority to academic institutions and government agencies, but low authority to commercial sites. Rieh (2002) also finds that the institutional level of source (such as institutional reputation) has a greater influence on the judgment of quality and authority than the individual level of source (such as author credential). A number of studies find that the criteria used in evaluating information on the Web are quite similar to those used in the print environment (Brandt, 1996; McMurdo, 1998). Fritch and Cromwell (2001) argue that many people fail to properly evaluate Web-based information largely due to a lack of understanding of authority. They attempt to provide a theoretical framework for assessing information on the Web with regard to cognitive authority.

We have witnessed a proliferation of less credible Web sites over the past few years. How to enhance the credibility of Web sites becomes one of the major challenges that Web designers are facing today. Researchers from the Stanford University Persuasive Technology Lab have published a series of studies related to Web credibility. These studies focus mostly on Web site elements (Fogg et al., 2000; Fogg et al., 2001; Stanford et al., 2002; Tseng and Fogg, 1999). For example, a recent study investigates how different elements of a Web site (e.g., links and domains) affect people's perception of credibility and discusses design implications (Fogg et al., 2001). Other studies examine factors that affect trust in e-commerce Web sites (Cheskin Research, 1999; 2000).

In the field of marketing, there are a number of studies on the believability of advertisements (Beltramini and Stafford, 1993; Maloney, 1994). These studies examine not only content but also certain attributes of advertisements. Factors influencing people's perception of credibility include the content of the advertisement, prior experience, reputation of the company that produces a product, and the third party certification. Personal sources of information are viewed as being more credible than nonpersonal sources.

In the field of journalism, news believability is usually measured by message content, source reputation, source credibility, and source bias (Austin and Dong, 1994). Even though none of the above studies focuses on the believability of scholarly information on the Web, the criteria employed by these studies do provide us a useful framework for studying attributes of document believability on the Web. Flanagin and Metzger (2000) find that Web-based information was deemed as credible as that obtained from televisions, radios, and magazines, but not as credible as newspaper information. Experienced Web users tend to verify Web-based information more stringently. Johnson and Kaye (1998) show that gender is significantly correlated with credibility perceptions. Female readers tend to assign higher credibility and trustworthiness to Web-based information than males.

It is widely recognized that failure to use accurate and credible information from the Web can have serious consequences. The issue of credibility of medical information has received widespread attention. Nearly 50% of Internet users go online to seek health-related information on the Web. Given the critical nature of the information, a number of researchers emphasize the need for credibility assessment of health-related information on the Web (Jadad and Gagliardi, 1998; Wathen and Burkell, 2002). Eysenbach et al. (2002) demonstrate that the problem of inaccurate information is not limited to the Web. It also exists in other sources such as television, magazines, and newspapers. Marton (2003) finds that women give highest credibility to health care practitioners among all kinds of information resources. Books are rated second highest, followed by pamphlets and fact sheets. Web-based bulletin boards and chat rooms receive the lowest credibility rating. Dutta-Bergman (2004) demonstrates the importance of message content (i.e., completeness) in shaping credibility perceptions where complete information is judged to be more credible than incomplete information.

Research on credibility represents one of the unusual areas of scholarly research that has attracted a great deal of attention among scholars from a wide range of disciplines.[1] Studies in Web design, marketing, mass communication, and health sciences provide useful parameters in measuring credibility; however, people tend to have different trust criteria in different spheres of their credibility judgment. Criteria used for assessing the credibility of an advertisement may not be the same as criteria used for evaluating other types of documents, such as scholarly information on the Web. On the other hand, while researchers in library and information science have begun to pay attention to users' perception of the credibility of Web information, the efforts have been far from systematic. It is presumed that criteria in relevance judgment accumulated from previous studies may not directly apply to criteria used in credibility assessment. More studies on factors influencing users' perception of the credibility of information on the Web are desperately needed.

Lynch (2001) believes that the integration of trust into information retrieval systems is inevitable. He notes, "If done properly, this will inform and empower users; if done incorrectly, it threatens to be a tremendously powerful engine of censorship and control over information access." This is a very important challenge that we are facing as we embark on the digital era. Understanding these issues could enable us to gain a better understanding that will eventually lead to the design of Web systems that effectively support people's assessment of the credibility of information on the Web (Rieh, 2002), and will "truly empower users to deal with an information environment that is characterized not only by information overload but active deception by information providers" (Lynch, 2001).

As previously mentioned, people tend to have different trust criteria in different spheres of their credibility judgment. Criteria used for assessing the credibility of an advertisement may not be the same as criteria used for evaluating other types of documents. In this chapter, we focus on investigating students' perception of the credibility of scholarly information on the Web. Undergraduate and graduate students were selected as the sampled population for the following reasons: They are likely to use scholarly information from the Web to do their assignments and conduct research, and therefore are heavily involved in credibility assessment. Previous studies examine credibility assessment by scholars and faculty (Herring, 2001; Rieh, 2002). However, credibility assessment of scholarly information by graduate and undergraduate students remains unclear. There is a pressing need to understand how these nonexpert groups use scholarly information from the Web to do assignments and conduct research.

People tend to employ multiple criteria in credibility assessment. In this chapter, a cluster of twenty questions was used to measure the dimensions of credibility.[2] A seven-point Likert-type scale for each of the twenty questions was used. This format allows respondents to select a response from "−3" (least credible) to "+3" (most credible).

The questionnaire, consisting of 20 simple questions, was designed with the goal of achieving a higher response rate. Moreover, in order to achieve a deeper understanding of factors influencing students' perception of the credibility of information on the Web, an optional section consisting of the following five questions was included to gather their open-ended thoughts related to credibility judgments:

- What are the three most important criteria you use in evaluating the credibility of scholarly information *on print media*?
- What are the three most important criteria you use in evaluating the credibility of scholarly information *on the Web*?
- When you assess the credibility of scholarly information on the Web, what features make the information *credible*?

- When you assess the credibility of scholarly information on the Web, what features make the information *less credible*?
- Under what circumstance, do you trust Web-based information?

CRITERIA IN CREDIBILITY ASSESSMENT

Early research on credibility investigates the relationship between source credibility and its persuasive impact. In general, people tend to be more persuaded by highly credible sources. Source expertise and trustworthiness are envisaged as two central attributes of source credibility (Hovland, Janis and Kelley, 1953; Hovland and Weiss, 1951). Expertise refers to a communicator's qualifications or ability, whereas trustworthiness is perceived as the communicator's motive to tell the truth. Past research further indicates several secondary dimensions of source credibility (e.g., dynamism) may also influence credibility judgments.

In the Web environment, expertise may be reflected in the information content, author's reputation and institutional affiliation, or markers of academic respectability (e.g., previous publication in a printed journal and posting on a well-respected Web site). Trustworthiness is associated with professionalism, a lack of commercial content, no apparent bias, and references by trusted sources. Dynamism may be reflected in layout, graphics and interactive features (Flanagin and Metzger, 2007; Metzger et al., 2003).

The information content scale is made up of the following four items. As Table 7.1 shows, there are strong positive responses on these four items, indicating that resonance with one's beliefs, novelty of information, trustworthiness, and good quality, all have a positive impact on credibility perception. When people evaluate the credibility of Web-based information, they tend to heavily rely on their personal knowledge. A recent survey by the OCLC (Online Computer Library Center, 2005) reveals that "common sense/personal knowledge" is the most commonly used method when people judge the trustworthiness of Web-based information. People are active perceivers of information. Credibility assessment is a cognitive process by which information is filtered and selected. According to a recent study conducted by Fogg et al.

Table 7.1
Information Content Scale

Items	Mean	Standard deviation
The document content is consistent with what I believe	1.13	1.32
The document contains a lot of interesting information	1.21	1.17
The document content is trustworthy	1.28	1.19
The document content is of good quality	1.25	0.99

Table 7.2
Authorship Scale

Items	Mean	Standard deviation
The author is affiliated with a prestigious institution	1.36	0.88
The author is a famous expert	0.91	1.27
The document has multiple authorships	0.60	1.29
I read articles by the author(s) in printed journals	0.86	1.34

(2001), quality and trustworthiness are positively related to credibility assessment. In addition to quality and trustworthiness, the present study finds that people tend to perceive information that is consistent with their prior beliefs as credible. Because of the very nature of scholarly information, novelty is viewed as a positive contributor to credibility.

When a user begins to judge the believability of a document, he/she is likely to make a decision based on certain indirect features (such as author's reputation and affiliation) as well as the document content. People tend to give greater credibility to a document that is written by a well-known author, or by an author affiliated with a prestigious institution. A recent survey by the Electronic Publishing Initiative at Columbia (EPIC) reveals that almost 75% of students report they take steps to evaluate the trustworthiness of Web-based information for coursework. Among those who take steps to evaluate Web-based information, slightly more than 50% rely on the reputation of the source. Over 18% determine the reliability of information based on the reputation of the author.

The scores for all four items in Table 7.2 are positive, ranging from 0.60 to 1.36. Author affiliation with a prestigious institution is considered as a more positive indicator of perceived credibility than an author who is a famous expert (1.36 vs. 0.91). This result is consistent with Rieh's (2002) findings. She finds that the Web users' judgments of quality and authority are influenced more by the institutional level of source than by the individual level. Freelance publications (no affiliation) are considered as less credible (see Table 7.6). The low value in the multiple authorship items is reported to have a weak effect on the credibility perception. Approximately 38% of the respondents in the survey report that multiple authorship is neutral in credibility assessment.

Stanford et al. (2002) find that experts carefully evaluate information while consumers tend to rely heavily on visual appeal in their credibility judgment. Eastin's (2001) study of credibility assessments of online health information indicates that dynamism, as reflected in Web site layout, color, and graphics, could also influence credibility judgments.

One notable item in Table 7.3 is the item on whether the Web document includes references. Inclusion of references is viewed as a strong positive factor leading to higher perceived credibility: an overwhelming majority of the

Table 7.3
Layout and Structure Scale

Items	Mean	Standard deviation
The document has nice layout	0.76	0.91
The document contains credentials of the author(s)	0.78	0.98
The document contains a picture of the author(s)	0.03	0.88
The document includes tables and graphs	0.16	0.47
The document includes references	1.63	1.17
The document is a long document	0.38	0.92
The document has typos	−1.41	1.12
The document contains links that do not work	−1.03	0.93

respondents in the survey (74.2%) report that including references is viewed as a positive indicator in credibility assessment. It is interesting to note that documents having a nice layout or containing credentials of the author(s) have a positive impact on credibility perceptions, even though the impact is not very strong (0.76 and 0.78, respectively). Robins and Holmes (2008) demonstrate that there is some correlation between aesthetics/design and credibility perceptions. However, it is acknowledged by the authors that "the question remains concerning exactly what features, elements or configurations of features, and elements of design impact credibility judgment and in what way."

The very low values in the other three items (0.03 with containing a picture of the authors, 0.16 with including tables and graphs, and 0.38 with a long document) show that these elements are reported to have little impact on the credibility perception. The negative values with typos (−1.41) and with broken links (−1.03) clearly indicate that they hurt the credibility perception.

According to Table 7.4, people give the greatest rating to documents that have been previously published in printed journals. Eighty-two percent of the respondents in the survey rate it positively in their credibility assessment.

Table 7.4
Web Site and Usage Scale

Items	Mean	Standard deviation
The document is posted on a well-respected Web site	1.46	1.15
The document was also published in a printed journal	1.71	1.24
The document is linked by a trusted source	1.18	1.26
The document contains a meter indicating the number of visits	−0.46	1.38

This is heavily influenced by their experience with print media, because most documents published in scholarly journals must go through a refereed process. Both documents hosted on a well-respected Web site and linked by a trusted source are viewed as a very positive attribute of credibility. These results are quite consistent with those presented in a recent joint study. In the Stanford et al. (2002) study, the survey items "The site is by an organization that is well-respected" and "The site is linked to by a site you think is believable" receive very high credibility rankings from experts and consumers. Documents with a meter showing the number of visits are reported to somewhat reduce credibility perception.

Among the twenty items in the survey, the two most positive contributors to credibility perceptions are "The document was also published in a printed journal" (1.71) and "The document includes references" (1.63), followed by "The document is hosted on a well-respected Web site" (1.46), and "The author is affiliated with a prestigious institution" (1.36). It seems that markers of academic respectability play a significant role in shaping students' credibility judgments. The two most negative factors leading to credibility perceptions are "The document has typos" (−1.41) and "The document contains links that do not work" (−1.03). It seems that the two most neutral items are "The document contains a picture of the author(s)" (0.03) and "The document includes tables and graphs" (0.16). More related information on features that impact the perceived credibility of scholarly information on the Web is summarized in Tables 7.5 and 7.6.

DOCUMENT FEATURES IN CREDIBILITY PERCEPTIONS

Similar to the context where people evaluate the relevance of information, people tend to employ multiple criteria simultaneously when they assess the credibility of information (Rieh and Belkin, 1998). Tables 7.5 and 7.6 present the results of optional questions completed by forty individuals who identify thirty-one credible features and twenty-five less-credible features, clearly indicating the diversity and complexity in credibility perceptions.

Although little comprehensive research has directly addressed the effect of document features on credibility perceptions, Tables 7.5 and 7.6 suggest certain document features may affect the perceived credibility. For instance, opinionated language (e.g., if the site seems subjective and uses words like "I" or "in my opinion") is reported as a negative attribute of credibility. This argument is consistent with a number of studies. Metzger et al. (2003) point out that "communicators who use more opinionated language in their messages are rated as less credible than those who use less intense language."

"Taking into account the views of other scholars" is listed as a credible feature. Similar findings have been reported in a recent study of the credibility of e-health information. Dutta-Bergman (2004) indicates that, "e-health

Table 7.5
Features Making the Information on the Web Credible

Information Content
- Resonance with personal knowledge/beliefs.
- The information is well.organized.
- Good-quality content.
- Good logic, spelling, and grammar.
- Not trying to sell something.
- Does not try to be "definite" answer on the subject matter.
- Taking into account the views of other scholars.
- No apparent bias.
- Writing on a standard academic level.

Authorship
- The author has publications/background in the subject area.
- Known author.
- Author affiliates with a prestigious institution.
- Clear information about who is posting the information and their goals.

Layouts and Structure
- Credentials of the author included.
- Fewer advertisements and pictures.
- Well documented (includes references).
- Clear layout.
- Working links.
- Agreement between sites (coincides with other sites' representations).

Web Sites and Usage
- Information is sponsored by a respected organization.
- Published in printed forms or presented at a conference.
- Linked by a credible source.
- URL domains such as edu.
- Referenced by reputable sources.
- Information is hosted on an official Web site.

Others
- Information verifiable somewhere else.
- Inclusion of contact information.
- Newly updated materials.
- Information is not free (needs subscription or purchase).
- Cited by other authors in other documents.
- Information has been evaluated by a librarian.

information was judged to be more credible when the information was complete as compared to instances when the information was incomplete."

Dynamism has been found to influence perceived credibility. Eastin (2001) notes: "When a message/presentation of a message is found to be highly dynamic, perceptions of source credibility are elevated." Document features

Table 7.6
Features Making the Information on the Web Less Credible

Information Content
- Lack of professionalism.
- Badly written/sloppy writing.
- Questionable statements/logic flaws.
- Factual errors.
- If the site seems subjective and uses words like "I" or "in my opinion."
- Author's beliefs differ from my own.

Authorship
- No author name is given.
- Freelance publication (no affiliation).

Layouts and Structure
- Poor layout and design.
- Absence of author credentials.
- Outdated links/bad links.
- Typos/spelling errors.
- Multiple colors.
- Color graphs.
- Strange fonts.
- Broken images.
- Presence of advertisements.
- No references included.

Web Sites and Usage
- Little information on who creates the Web site.
- Hosted on unknown or freely available Web host.
- Lack of edu domain.
- Obscure domain names.
- Linked by a questionable or commercial site.

Others
- If the author or sponsoring organization will benefit financially by the spread of the information.
- Sites not recently updated.

such as "working links" and "newly updated materials" are deemed as characteristics of credibility.

Presence of commercial motives (e.g., selling intent, presence of advertising, and linked by a questionable or commercial site) bothers students in this survey, consistent with studies indicating that people tend to discount information with obvious commercial motives. Flanagin and Metzger's study (2000) shows that commercial information is perceived as having the lowest credibility of several types of information. Lasica (2002) also finds that "paid links" can reduce the credibility of a site or an article.

When people evaluate the credibility of scholarly information on print media, criteria such as the publisher (or journal), author's affiliation and reputation, and content are commonly used. Similar criteria are reported when they assess the credibility of scholarly information on the Web such as institutions that host the Web site, author's affiliation and reputation, and content. The criteria used in evaluating scholarly information on the Web do not seem very different from the print media (Burton and Chadwick, 2000). However, since most scholarly information on the Web does not go through a refereed process, more efforts are required to evaluate it. In such a large uncontrolled environment, students tend to pay special attention to the following issues:

- Does the document include verifiable sources (e.g., citations, references, and author's contact information such as e-mail address)?

- Has the information been evaluated by other people? Because of the absence of a refereed process with most scholarly information on the Web, when students do the credibility assessment, they tend to defer judgments to others whom they trust. They pay great attention to the following issues: Is the document linked by a credible source? Do other authors in other documents cite the information? Has the information been evaluated by a librarian? Has the information been presented at a conference or published in a printed journal? (See also Table 7.5.)

- Typos and grammatical errors in printed journals are seen not as common as in the Web environment. Because of the self-publishing nature of most scholarly information on the Web, people tend to be very sensitive to typos and grammatical errors when they evaluate the credibility of scholarly information on the Web (see also Tables 7.3 and 7.6).

- Because of the dynamic nature of the Web, people also look at aspects such as broken links, sites not recently updated, and multiple colors (see also Table 7.6).

TYPES OF SOURCE CREDIBILITY

Tseng and Fogg (1999) identify the following four types of source credibility in assessing information on the Web: presumed credibility (e.g., stereotypes), reputed credibility (e.g., source labels and official titles), surface credibility (e.g., simple inspection of a book cover), and experienced credibility (e.g., judgment based on prior experience). These four types of source credibility also provide a useful theoretical framework for understanding user's perceptions of credibility of scholarly information on the Web, such as information hosted on a well-respected Web site (presumed credibility); author's affiliation with a prestigious institution (reputed credibility); document layout (surface credibility); and publication of the same document in a printed journal (experienced credibility).

In addition to the four types of source credibility identified by Tseng and Fogg (1999), this study shows that two other types of source credibility play a significant role in shaping students' perceptions of credibility.

- Verifiable credibility:

Eastin (2001) points out that "anyone can publish and thus disseminate online information under any name, reducing the reliability of putative source as a usable heuristic cue." This new problem highlights the importance of verification in the online environment. As Table 7.3 shows, documents including references have a significant positive impact on credibility perception. Documents that are evaluated, cited, linked, or published in printed journals are also perceived as credible (see Table 7.5). Likewise, absence of authors and lack of contact information represent less-credible features (see Table 7.6). It seems that students may not be as well equipped as scholars or experts to make credibility assessment. Students therefore look for verifiable sources to confirm their credibility appraisal. Similarly, other studies show that presence of a "physical" address, contact phone number, and e-mail address increases the credibility of online information (Fogg et al., 2001; Freeman and Spyridakis, 2004).

- Cost-effort credibility:

Credibility is a very complex concept. A cluster of only twenty questions makes it impossible to capture every single dimension of credibility. An optional section with five open-ended questions was designed to capture some unexpected issues. It is interesting to find that two students who completed the optional questions raised cost-effort issues. Like other studies, presence of advertisements hurts the credibility perception because of commercial motives. Web-based information that is not free and needs a subscription or purchase is, however, viewed as credible (see Table 7.5). It is very easy to access free scholarly information on the Web. The ease in accessing free scholarly information may have an impact on credibility perception. People may take free information from the Web for granted. Documents that require effort to obtain them or that require subscription fees are more likely to be considered as credible documents.

Trust is pervasive in the digital environment. People's trust in digital media is also shaped by their expectations and experience with print media (see Chapter 4). In the traditional print environment, scholarly publications need to go through a refereed process, and are usually available through subscription or purchase, or through libraries. This may be the reason why cost-effort plays an important role in shaping credibility perception.

CIRCUMSTANCES AFFECTING CREDIBILITY ASSESSMENT

Scholars have found that perceptions of credibility can be highly situational. Factors such as motivations of information seekers, information overload, and constraints caused by evaluative contexts can significantly influence credibility assessments (Rieh and Danielson, 2007). For example, Rosenthal (1971) notes that information that cannot be validated would be deemed as less credible. Flanagin and Metzger (2000) indicate that people's perceptions of credibility also depend on the context in which information will be used such as news and entertainment.

Credibility assessment is not a perfectionist endeavor; it inevitably entails judgments about the degree of credibility one needs (Burbules, 2001). Therefore, people's perception of credibility of scholarly information on the Web is also contextual. For example, time constraints may make serious evaluations impractical. Students may take a more rigorous and serious approach to examine materials used for their doctoral dissertations. However, students are less likely to go beyond the surface features when they evaluate materials used for an assignment that is due on the following day.

Circumstances that seem to affect students' willingness to accept scholarly information on the Web are identified as follows:

- The immediacy with which users need to use the information.
- The (lack of) availability of the information elsewhere.
- The consistency of the information with users' prior beliefs or knowledge.
- The verifiability of the information through other means.
- The acceptance of the information in the academic community.
- The presence of the information on multiple respected Web sites.
- The recommendation of the information by experts.
- The dissemination of the information by highly authoritative institutions.
- The availability of the information in an academic database.

CONCLUSION

Freeman and Spyridakis (2004) state that "many readers of online information rarely spend the time to research the credibility of the publisher or author of information in Web pages they read. By default, many readers tend to judge information on a given Web page only by the information on that page. Therefore they may gauge the credibility of information on a Web page on the basis of peripheral cues on a Web page, such as the presence and absence of a street address." Library and information professionals are becoming increasingly aware of the need to educate users about how to effectively find good information on the Web. Understanding factors influencing students' perceptions of the credibility of scholarly information on the Web would enable us to improve user education, and eventually better inform and empower users. In the digital environment, one of the new responsibilities of information professionals is to facilitate people's judgments about the credibility of information.

This chapter also has practical implications for Web system design, such as credibility ranking systems to permit users to factor trust preferences about the information on the Web. At present, identifying credible information is left to users, who sift through results lists and make quick judgments (Toms and Taves, 2004). When users retrieve a huge number of relevant documents from the Web, most of them view only a small number that are displayed at the beginning (e.g., first 100–200 documents). It would be very helpful to display most credible documents first so that users would not miss credible documents. Another approach is to highlight certain credibility features to support efficient credibility assessment. For example, when users evaluate the credibility of Web-based information, most of them may look at certain information elements (e.g., references, institutional affiliations, and URL domains). Highlighting these information elements may facilitate users' appraisal of credibility.

This chapter attempts to explore students' perception of credibility of information in a large uncontrolled Web environment. It should be noted here that what students perceive may not always be accurate. In fact, none of us can be entirely immune to this weakness. It would be very critical to investigate evaluation errors (Tseng and Fogg, 1999) such as "gullibility error" (i.e., information is not credible, but users perceive it to be credible) and "incredulity error" (i.e., credible information is wrongly rejected).

This chapter attempts to identify factors that affect students' credibility assessment as a group. Another possible way of research might be to look at how the level of expertise (e.g., faculty, graduate, and undergraduate students) affects their credibility assessments. Studies have shown that experienced Internet users may act differently than less experienced users in credibility judgments (Freeman and Spyridakis, 2004; Johnson and Kaye, 2002). It seems important to find out how novice and experienced users differ in evaluating the credibility of scholarly information on the Web.

Future research can also extend the findings of this study by investigating similar research problems with different types of information, or in different cultural contexts. The following chapter will take a closer look at how students in a different culture make credibility assessments of Web-based information for their research, and what evaluation criteria they employ. Similarities and differences in credibility assessment between American and Chinese students will also be discussed.

Improvement in information technologies enables us to gather, store, and transmit information in a vast quantity, but not to interpret it. Perhaps, what is most needed is more intelligent technologies that could help us make sense of the growing volume of information. Assessing the credibility of information in the distributed environment is a very complex process. Some aspects of information credibility are within our control while others are not. Future research could focus on *reducing* rather than *eliminating* users' cognitive efforts in identifying whether a document is believable or not.

NOTES

1. For comprehensive reviews of literature related to the credibility of information, please see Metzger et al. (2003), Rieh and Danielson (2007), and Wathen and Burkell (2002). Stanford University Persuasive Technology Lab also maintains a Web site related to the literature on Web credibility (please see http://credibility.stanford.edu/resources.html). Self's (1996) chapter offers an excellent historical overview of credibility research.

2. How was the survey conducted? Two hundred and fifty copies of the questionnaires were distributed to students at San Jose State University, California, either in class, at the library, or at the student center during the spring of 2003. Participants in this study are undergraduate and graduate students from diverse disciplines such as computer science, engineering, business administration, and library and information science. Participants were asked to fill out the questionnaires based on their experience in selecting Web-based information for research purposes, and to complete the optional open-ended questions, if possible. One hundred and thirty-five returned copies include 128 completed questionnaires and seven incomplete questionnaires. The results of these 128 completed questionnaires are presented in Tables 7.1–7.4. These 128 completed questionnaires also include forty completed copies of the optional section. Results from forty individuals who completed the optional questions are summarized in Tables 7.5–7.6.

REFERENCES

Austin, E.W. and Dong, Q. (1994). Source v. Content Effects on Judgments of News Believability. *Journalism Quarterly*, 71(4), 973–983.

Beltramini, R.F. and Stafford, E.R. (1993). Comprehension and Perceived Believability of Seals of Approval Information in Advertising. *Journal of Advertising*, 22 (3), 3–13.

Brandt, D.S. (1996). Evaluating Information on the Internet. *Computers in Libraries*, 16(5), 44–46.

Buckland, M. and Plaunt, C. (1997). Selecting Libraries, Selecting Documents, Selecting Data. Retrieved December 30, 2007, from http://people.ischool.berkeley.edu/~buckland/isdl97/isdl97.html.

Burbules, N.C. (2001). Paradoxes of the Web: The Ethical Dimensions of Credibility. *Library Trends*, 49(3), 441–453.

Burton, V. and Chadwick, S. (2000). Investigating the Practices of Student Researchers: Pattern of Use and Criteria for Use of Internet and Library Sources. *Computers and Composition*, 17(3), 309.

Cheskin Research (1999). e-Commerce Trust Study. Retrieved March 3, 2003, from *http://studioarchetype.com/headlines/etrust_frameset.html*.

Cheskin Research (2000). Trust in the Wired Americas. Retrieved March 3, 2003, from *http://www.cheskin.com/thinkk/studies/trust2.html*.

Dutta-Bergman, M.J. (2004). The Impact of Completeness and Web Use Motivation on the Credibility of e-Health Information. *Journal of Communication*, 54(2), 253–269.

Eastin, M.S. (2001). Credibility Assessments of Online Health Information: The Effects of Source Expertise and Knowledge of Content. *Journal of Computer-Mediated Communication*, 6(4). Retrieved November 3, 2007, from http://www.ascusc.org/jcmc/vol6/issue4/eastin.html.

The Electronic Publishing Initiative at Columbia (EPIC) Online Survey of College Students: Executive Summary. Retrieved February 3, 2008, from http://epic.columbia.edu/eval/find09/find09.html.

Eysenbach, G., Powell, J., Kuss, O., and Sa, E.R. (2002). Empirical Studies Assessing the Quality of Health Information for Consumers on the World Wide Web: A Systematic Review. *Journal of the American Medical Association*, 287(20), 2691–2700.

Fiske, A.P. (1991). *Structures of Social Life: The Four Elementary Forms of Human Relations: Communal Sharing, Authority Ranking, Equality Matching, Market Pricing*. New York, NY: Free Press.

Flanagin, A.J. and Metzger, M.J. (2000). Perceptions Of Internet Information Credibility. *Journalism and Mass Communication Quarterly*, 77(3), 515–540.

Flanagin, A.J. and Metzger, M.J. (2007). The Role Of Site Features, User Attributes, And Information Verification Behaviors On The Perceived Credibility Of Web-Based Information. *New Media & Society*, 9(2), 319–342.

Fogg, B.J., Marshall, J., Laraki, O., Osipovich, A., Varma, C., Fang, N., Paul, J., Rangnekar, A., Shon, J., Swani, P., and Treinen, M. (2001). What Makes Web Sites Credible? In *Proceedings of ACM CHI 2001 Conference on Human Factors in Computing Systems* (pp. 61–68). New York, NY: ACM Press.

Fogg, B.J., Swani, P., Treinen, M., Marshall, J., Osipovich, A., Varma, C., Laraki, O., Fang, N., Paul, J., Rangnekar, A., and Shon, J. (2000). Elements that Affect Web Credibility: Early Results for a Self-Report Study. In *Proceedings of ACM CHI 2000 Conference on Human Factors in Computing Systems* (pp. 287–288). New York, NY: ACM Press.

Freeman, K.S. and Spyridakis, J.H. (2004). An Examination of Factors that Affect the Credibility of Online Health Information. *Technical Communication*, 51(2), 239–263.

Fritch, J.W. and Cromwell, R.L. (2001). Evaluating Internet Resources: Identity, Affiliation, and Cognitive Authority in a Networked World. *Journal of the American Society for Information Science and Technology*, 52(6), 499–507.

Gunther, A.C. (1992). Biased Press or Biased Public? Attitudes Toward Media Coverage of Social Groups. *Public Opinion Quarterly*, 56(2), 147–167.

Hawkins, S.D. (1999). What is Credible Information? *Online*, 23(5), 213–219.

Healy, J.M. (1990). *Endangered Minds: Why Our Children Don't Think*. New York, NY: Simon and Schuster.

Herring, S.D. (2001). Using the World Wide Web for Research: Are Faculty Satisfied? *Journal of Academic Librarianship*, 27(3), 213–219.

Hovland, C.I., Janis, I.L., and Kelly, H.H. (1953). *Communication and Persuasion*. New Haven, CT: Yale University Press.

Hovland, C.I. and Weiss, W. (1951). The Influence of Source Credibility on Communication Effectiveness. *Public Opinion Quarterly*, 15(4), 635–650.

Jadad, A.R. and Gagliardi, A. (1998). Rating Health Information on the Internet: Navigating to Knowledge or to Babel? *Journal of the American Medical Association*, 279(8), 611–614.

Johnson, T.J. and Kaye, B.K. (1998). Cruising is Believing? Comparing Internet and Traditional Sources on Media Credibility Measures. *Journal of Mass Communication Quarterly*, 75(2), 325–340.

Johnson, T.J. and Kaye, B.K. (2002). Webelievability: A path model examining how convenience and reliance predict online credibility. *Journalism & Mass Communication Quarterly*, 79(3), 619–642.

Lasica, J.D. (2002, April). Online News: Credibility Gap Ahead? *Online Journalism Review*. Retrieved November 3, 2007, from http://www.ojr.org/ojr/lasica/1019079841.php.

Lynch, C.A. (2001). When Documents Deceive: Trust and Provenance as New Factors for Information Retrieval in a Tangled Web. *Journal of the American Society for Information Science and Technology*, 52(1), 12–17.

Maloney, J.C. (1994). Is Advertising Believability Really Important? *Marketing Management*, 3(1), 47–52.

Marton, C. (2003). Quality of Health Information on the Web: User Perceptions of Relevance and Reliability. *The New Review of Information Behaviour Research*, 4(1), 195–206.

McMurdo, G. (1998). Evaluating Web Information and Design. *Journal of Information Science*, 24(3), 192–204.

Metzger, M.J., Flanagin, A.J., Eyal, K., Lemus, D.R., and McCann, R. (2003). Credibility in the 21st Century: Integrating Perspectives on Source, Message, and Media Credibility in the Contemporary Media Environment. In P. Kalbfleisch (Ed.), *Communication Yearbook* (Vol. 27, pp. 293–335). Mahwah, NJ: Lawrence Erlbaum.

Meyrowitz, J. (1985). *No Sense of Place: The Impact of Electronic Media on Social Behavior*. New York, NY: Oxford University Press.

OCLC (2005). *Perceptions of Library and Information Resources*. Dublin, OH: OCLC. Retrieved January 3, 2008, from http://www.oclc.org/reports/2005perceptions.htm.

Rieh, S.Y. (2002). Judgment of Information Quality and Cognitive Authority in the Web. *Journal of the American Society for Information Science and Technology*, 53(2), 145–161.

Rieh, S.Y. and Belkin, N.J. (1998). Understanding Judgment of Information Quality and Cognitive Authority in the WWW. In C.M. Preston (Ed.), *Proceedings of the 61st ASIS Annual Meeting* (pp. 279–289). Silver Spring, MD: American Society for Information Science.

Rieh, S.Y. and Danielson, D.R. (2007). Credibility: A Multidisciplinary Framework. In B. Cronin (Ed.), *Annual Review of Information Science and Technology* (Vol. 41, pp. 307–364). Medford, NJ: Information Today.

Robins, D. and Holmes, J. (2008). Aesthetics and Credibility in Web Site Design. *Information Processing and Management*, 44(1), 386–399.

Rosenthal, P.I. (1971). Specificity, Verifiability and Message Credibility. *Quarterly Journal of Speech*, 57, 393–401.

Self, C.C. (1996). Credibility. In: M.B. Salven and D.W. Stacks (Eds.), *An Integrated Approach to Communication Theory and Research* (pp. 421–441). Mahwah, NJ: Lawrence Erlbaum Associates.

Stanford, J., Tauber, E., Fogg, B.J., and Marable, L. (2002). Experts vs. Online Consumers: A Comparative Credibility Study of Health and Finance Web Sites. Retrieved February 23, 2008, from http://www.consumerwebwatch. org/dynamic/web-credibility-reports-experts-vs-online-abstract.cfm.

Toms, E.G. and Taves, A.R. (2004). Measuring User Perceptions of Web Site Reputation. *Information Processing and Management*, 40(2), 291–317.

Tseng, S. and Fogg, B.J. (1999). Credibility and Computing Technology. *Communications of the ACM*, 42(5), 39–44.

Wathen, C.N., and Burkell, J. (2002). Believe it or Not: Factors Influencing Credibility on the Web. *Journal of the American Society for Information Science and Technology*, 53(2), 134–144.

8

———•◦•◦•———

CULTURAL DIFFERENCES IN CREDIBILITY ASSESSMENT

The advent of the Internet has made a plethora of information available online on almost every imaginable topic. The shift from physical to online access raises new concerns among librarians and faculty about how students evaluate and use Web-based information. Kandell (1998) points out that "college students as a group appear more vulnerable to developing a dependence on the Internet than most segments of society."

Because of the deluge of misinformation online, coupled with a relative lack of experience, making appraisals of the credibility of information becomes a challenging task for most young information seekers. Scholz-Crane's (1998) study also shows that few college students exert a great deal of effort in rigorously assessing Web-based information.

High school and college students frequently turn first to the Web for school-related tasks (Tenopir, 2003). However, most of them are not aware of the distinctions between materials on the Web and peer-reviewed journals. Graham and Metaxas (2003) find that many undergraduate students use the Internet as a primary source of information, usually with little regard to the accuracy of that information. Grimes and Boening (2001) also warn that there is an ever-increasing number of students using unevaluated Internet information at the expense of traditional print materials. Friedlander (2002) finds that 75.4% of the respondents agree with the statement—"The Internet provides high-quality information"—and 45.9% of the respondents are using

This chapter is an updated and expanded version of an earlier article: Liu, Z. and Huang, X. (2005). Evaluating the Credibility of Scholarly Information on the Web: A Cross Cultural Study. *International Information & Library Review*, 37(2), 99–106.

Internet information without any additional verification. A study by Kelley and Orr (2003) reveals that a large percentage of students at the University of Maryland University College (UMUC) use the free Web frequently, highlighting the need of library's instructional programs to teach students about how to evaluate and use Web-based information. They find that the majority of students prefer conducting a search on the free Web because using a library is likely to be more difficult and time-consuming.

The Online Computer Library Center (OCLC) white paper on the information habits of college students (2002) shows that college students are confident in their abilities to evaluate information on the Web for course assignments. They make their own decisions about which information to use, unless their instructors or teaching assistants direct them to specific course-related Web sites. In a survey of faculty satisfaction of the Internet as a research source, Herring (2001) finds that although faculty welcome the vast quantity of information, many of them are concerned about the reliability and accuracy of Internet information. Faculty members from science disciplines tend to be more positive about the reliability of Web-based information than do faculty in the social sciences, or language and literature areas.

Cross-cultural comparisons with regard to the perception of Web credibility have begun receiving attention. Fogg et al. (2001) find that respondents from Finland report lower credibility rating for Web sites that convey commercial implications. However, compared to Finns, respondents in the United States assign higher credibility to Web sites using tailoring technology and those that convey expertise and trustworthiness. Dong (2003) examines the use of Internet information from the perspective of Chinese students and scholars. She finds that the younger generation with advanced degrees tend to spend more time on the Internet and give higher evaluation ratings on the usefulness of Internet information. She also finds that accuracy and authority are the most important factors when users judge the quality of Web-based information.

The arrival of the Internet has a significant impact on the way people gather information for research around the world. Studies of students' credibility assessment have not kept pace. Most previous studies examine credibility assessment by scholars and students in the United States (Herring, 2001; Rieh, 2002). However, credibility assessment of scholarly information from people in other cultures remains largely unexplored. Credibility perception is deeply embedded in and heavily influenced by social and cultural contexts. Cultural differences may have a strong impact on credibility assessment. This creates a pressing need to understand how people from different cultures use scholarly information from the Web to do assignments and conduct research.

The World Wide Web (WWW) is becoming a pervasive resource for scholars and students in China. Credibility assessment is increasingly important as scholars and students use the Web to carry out a variety of research activities. According to a recent study (Dong, 2003), "research papers" and "latest developments" are reported as the two most heavily accessed information resources from the Web by scholars and students in China. Like students in other countries, students in China are also faced with decisions about the Internet information they choose to use for their research.

In this chapter, we attempt to find out how undergraduate and graduate students in China make credibility assessments, the evaluation criteria they use, and the similarities and differences in the credibility assessment between Chinese undergraduate and graduate students. Given the Western orientation of most previous studies, we also explore the similarities and differences in credibility evaluation between American and Chinese students. We attempt to answer these questions by conducting a comparative study of undergraduate and graduate students in China.[1,2] Then we compare these results with the survey results in Chapter 7.

The survey questions in this parallel study are based on those in Chapter 7. A variable is added in order to examine how Chinese students perceive credibility of information hosted on a Web site in an advanced country when they are doing credibility judgments. Stereotypes are cognitive structures that contain accumulated knowledge and beliefs about particular social groups. Expectancies about others are often based on stereotypes of groups to which they belong. As noted by Hamilton, Sherman, and Ruvolo (1990), "stereotype-based expectancies can influence the way we process the information we receive, seek additional information, and guide our behavioral interactions with others. These processes have important functional values as we adapt to our social world. In addition, however, they present the potential for bias and hence the opportunity for error." People in credibility assessment are active information seekers instead of passive information receivers. Stereotype-based expectations can influence credibility assessment in several ways. Stereotype-based expectations may lead people to focus on certain kinds of information while ignoring other kinds. For example, stereotype-based expectations may result in people in developing countries blindly valuing information from certain highly developed countries while ignoring valuable information from developing countries. Therefore, a cross-cultural analysis of credibility assessment should deal with stereotype-based expectations.

CREDIBILITY ASSESSMENT: UNDERGRADUATE VERSUS GRADUATE STUDENTS IN CHINA

Students use a variety of strategies in evaluating scholarly information on the Web, such as checking the document content and structure, identifying the author's qualifications or institutions that host the information on the Web, looking at document outlook, and checking whether the information is linked by a trusted source.

The first four variables are related to credibility perceptions of information content. According to Table 8.1, there are very positive responses on

Table 8.1
Credibility Assessment by Chinese Students

Variables	Graduate (Mean)	Undergraduate (Mean)	Difference
1. The document content is consistent with what I believe	1.42	1.27	0.15
2. The document contains a lot of interesting information	0.73	0.72	0.01
3. The document content is trustworthy	1.50	1.25	0.25
4. The document content is of good quality	1.05	1.30	0.25
5. The author is affiliated with a prestigious institution	0.89	0.96	0.07
6. The author is a famous expert	0.90	1.06	0.16
7. The document has multiple authorship	0.81	0.63	0.18
8. I read articles by the author(s) in printed journals	1.05	0.82	0.23
9. The document has a nice layout	0.50	0.72	0.22
10. The document contains credentials of the author(s)	0.47	1.04	0.57
11. The document contains a picture of the author(s)	0.18	−0.10	0.28
12. The document includes tables and graphs	1.11	0.96	0.15
13. The document includes references	1.66	1.46	0.20
14. The document is a long document	0.59	0.93	0.34
15. The document contains links that do not work	−0.54	−0.69	0.15
16. The document is hosted on a Web site in an advanced country	0.03	0.54	0.51
17. The document is posted on a well-respected Web site	1.24	1.54	0.30
18. The document was also published in a printed journal	1.56	1.23	0.33
19. The document is linked by a trusted source	1.20	1.08	0.12
20. The document contains a meter indicating the number of visits	0.38	0.46	0.08

variables 1, 3, and 4, indicating that resonance with one's beliefs, trustworthiness, and quality are deemed as positive contributors to credibility by both undergraduate and graduate students in China. Documents containing a lot of interesting information (variable 2) add credibility, even though the impact is weak (0.73 for graduate and 0.72 for undergraduate students).

Variables 5–8 assess the importance of authorship. All scores are positive, ranging from 0.81 to 1.05 for graduate and from 0.63 to 1.06 for undergraduate students. This indicates that both groups view the reputation of authors, institutional affiliation, and multiple authorship as positive indicators of credibility. In a similar study of credibility perceptions by American students, Chapter 7 shows that author affiliation with a prestigious institution is considered a more positive credibility indicator than an author who is a famous expert (1.36 vs. 0.91), and freelance publications (no affiliation) are perceived as less credible. Rieh (2002) also finds that Web users' judgments of quality and authority are influenced more by the institutional level of source than by the individual level. Table 8.1 shows that there are no significant differences in credibility rankings between institutional affiliation (variable 5) and author's reputation (variable 6) by these two groups of Chinese students.

Variables 9–15 pertain to the impact of document layout and structure on credibility assessment. Both groups view documents providing references as a strong positive contributor to credibility, and documents containing broken links as a negative factor leading to reduced credibility. Undergraduate students tend to value attractive layouts, inclusion of credentials, and length of documents more than graduate students. However, graduate students assign higher credibility ratings to documents containing the author's picture as well as tables and graphs than do undergraduate students.

Variables 16–20 are mostly related to Web site reputation and usage. Both groups give high credibility ratings to documents hosted on a well-respected Web site, linked by a trusted source, or published in a printed journal. Documents containing a visit meter (variable 20) are perceived as somewhat positive by both groups of students. It is interesting to note that undergraduate students assign a higher value to documents hosted in an advanced country Web site than do graduate students (0.54 for undergraduate and 0.03 for graduate students).

Among the twenty variables in this survey, the two most significant differences in credibility rating between graduate and undergraduate students are "The document contains credentials of the author(s)" (0.57) and "The document is hosted on a Web site in an advanced country" (0.51), followed by "The document is a long document" (0.34). It seems that presumed credibility, reputed credibility, and surface credibility have a stronger impact on undergraduate students than on graduate students in credibility assessment.

Another notable difference between the two groups of students is in variable 18, "The document was also published in a printed journal." Documents published in printed journals add credibility for undergraduate students (1.23), but are even more for graduate students (1.56). This indicates that graduate students value experienced credibility more than undergraduate students.

The criteria used in evaluating scholarly information on the Web do not seem very different from the print media. When students evaluate the credibility of scholarly information on the Web, they frequently focus on criteria

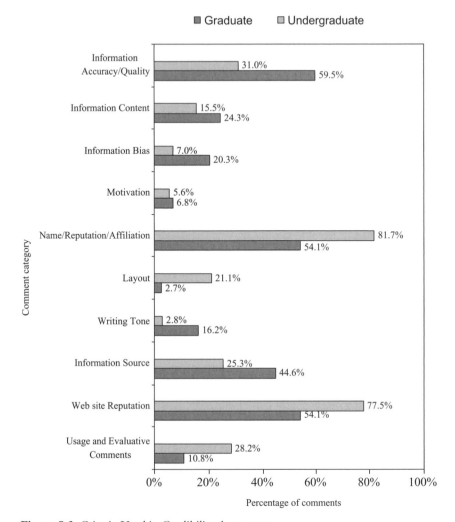

Figure 8.1 Criteria Used in Credibility Assessment.

such as institutions that host the Web site, author's affiliation/reputation, as well as content. Figure 8.1 compares comments from undergraduate and graduate students on the three most important criteria used in credibility evaluation. The three most frequently used criteria by these two groups are quite similar: information accuracy/quality, author's name/reputation/affiliation, and Web site reputation. However, the groups differ greatly in the extent of employing these three criteria. Undergraduate students predominantly rely on author's name/reputation/affiliation as well as Web site reputation for their credibility assessments, and they cite a lot more than graduate students on author's name/reputation/affiliation (81.7% vs. 54.1%) and Web site reputation (77.5% vs. 54.1%). In contrast, graduate students focus more than undergraduate students on information accuracy/quality (59.5% vs. 31.0%).

Figure 8.1 also shows that graduate students tend to pay more attention than undergraduate students to information content, information bias, writing tone, and information sources. However, undergraduate students rely more than graduate students on layout as well as usage and evaluative comments made by others. This finding is further confirmed by another recent study. In a comparison of how experts and consumers evaluate the same health and finance sites, Stanford and other researchers (2002) find that experts evaluate content carefully while consumers tend to rely on visual appeal for much of their credibility appraisal. It seems that levels of expertise may affect credibility assessment. Undergraduate students (especially first and second-year students) are more likely to seek evaluative comments made by others to confirm their judgments. Documents not recommended by experts or those that received bad reviews are considered less credible (see Table 8.3). Undergraduate students are also more likely to rely more on factors related to reputation (e.g., author's reputation and affiliation, Web site reputation) than to evaluate the content.

CREDIBILITY PERCEPTION: AMERICAN STUDENTS VERSUS CHINESE STUDENTS

Table 8.2 compares data of mean credibility ratings of graduate and undergraduate students in China with those made by U.S. students. It is interesting to note that the following variables are deemed the three most credible indicators by students in both countries:

- The document includes references.
- The document is posted on a well-respected Web site.
- The document was also published in a printed journal.

In addition, students in both countries assign similar credibility ratings to the variables, such as "The document content is trustworthy," "The document content is of good quality," "The document contains credentials of the author(s)," "The document contains a picture of the author(s)," and "The document is linked by a trusted source."

A number of notable differences exist in credibility rating between Chinese and American students:

1. Documents with visit meters are perceived as somewhat positive by Chinese students (0.42) while considered as somewhat negative by their American counterparts (−0.46). One possible explanation is that Chinese students tend to focus on the usage of the documents while American students are concerned with the motive

Table 8.2
Credibility Perceptions: American Students versus Chinese Students

Variables	Chinese students (Mean)	American students* (Mean)	Difference
1. The document content is consistent with what I believe	1.34	1.13	0.21
2. The document contains a lot of interesting information	0.72	1.21	0.49
3. The document content is trustworthy	1.38	1.28	0.10
4. The document content is of good quality	1.17	1.25	0.08
5. The author is affiliated with a prestigious institution	0.92	1.36	0.44
6. The author is a famous expert	0.98	0.91	0.07
7. The document has multiple authorship	0.72	0.60	0.12
8. I read articles by the author(s) in printed journals	0.94	0.86	0.08
9. The document has a nice layout	0.61	0.76	0.15
10. The document contains credentials of the author(s)	0.75	0.78	0.03
11. The document contains a picture of the author(s)	0.04	0.03	0.01
12. The document includes tables and graphs	1.03	0.16	0.87
13. The document includes references	1.57	1.63	0.06
14. The document is a long document	0.76	0.38	0.38
15. The document contains links that do not work	−0.61	−1.03	0.42
16. The document is hosted on a Web site in an advanced country	0.28	NA	NA
17. The document is posted on a well-respected Web site	1.39	1.46	0.07
18. The document was also published in a printed journal	1.39	1.71	0.32
19. The document is linked by a trusted source	1.14	1.18	0.04
20. The document contains a meter indicating the number of visits	0.42	−0.46	0.92

* *Note*: Data of American students are derived from Chapter 7.

for showing the number of visits (see also Figure 8.1). According to Table 8.3, Chinese students list low usage as a less credible feature.

2. Another notable difference between American and Chinese students is in the "The document includes tables and graphs" variable, where Chinese students give greater credibility to documents including tables and graphs than their American counterparts (Chinese 1.03 vs. American 0.16). It is also interesting to note that long documents are perceived as more credible by Chinese students than by American students (Chinese 0.76 vs. American 0.38). Perhaps from the Chinese perspective, these features are indicative of serious scholarly works. One respondent notes that good quality scholarly works are always supported by strong data or theories. Short papers and papers lacking in detailed information are perceived as less credible features by Chinese students (see Table 8.3).

3. Students in both countries show positive perceptions of documents containing a lot of interesting information; however, American students tend to perceive documents containing interesting information as more credible than do Chinese students (American 1.21 vs. Chinese 0.72). It seems that Chinese students are more critical of document content. Extreme and exaggerating content is described as less credible attributes by Chinese students (see Table 8.3). It is interesting to note that "constantly changing content" is listed as a less credible feature by Chinese students. It seems that the lack of communicative stability hurts credibility perceptions, probably because students believe constantly changing content is skeptical or too elusive to be trusted.

4. The document that contains links that do not work is perceived as more negative by American students (−1.03) than by Chinese students (−0.61). It would seem that Chinese students are more tolerant of documents with broken links than their American counterparts.

CONCLUSION

The immense amount of information readily available from the Web holds great promises as well as presents unprecedented challenges. Because of the ephemeral nature and the lack of a traditional refereed process, selecting credible information from the sheer amount of information has become a daunting task for most users. As Metzger, Flanagin, and Zwarun (2003) state: "Students need accurate, timely information from which to learn, but if they are faced with information that is inaccurate or misleading, and they lack the ability to distinguish this information from more credible sources, their learning is compromised. They may mistake erroneous or biased information for fact, and they may perpetuate such error or bias in their own work." Therefore, teaching users how to effectively evaluate and use Web-based information becomes an important educational objective for learners of all ages (Burbules, 2001). There is an increasing awareness among library and information professionals of the need to educate users on how to evaluate Internet information. Understanding credibility assessment in different cultural contexts would enable library and information professionals to improve user education and serve user needs more responsively.

Table 8.3
Less Credible Features Perceived by American and Chinese Students

By American students only*	By *both* American and Chinese students*	By Chinese students only
• If the site seems subjective and uses words like "I" or "in my opinion" • Multiple colors • Color graphs • Strange fonts • Broken images • Hosted on unknown or freely available Web host • Lack of edu domain • Linked by a questionable or commercial site • If the author or sponsoring organization will benefit financially by the spread of the information	• *Lack of professionalism* • *Badly written/sloppy writing* • *Questionable statements/ logic flaws* • *Factual errors* • *Author's beliefs differ from my own* • *No author name is given* • *Freelance publication (no affiliation)* • *Poor layout and design* • *Absence of author credentials* • *Outdated links/bad links* • *Typos/spelling errors* • *Presence of advertisements* • *No references included* • *Little information on who creates the Web site* • *Obscure domain names* • *Sites not recently updated*	• Exaggerated content • Repetitive content • Biased content • Constantly changing content • Ideas cannot be found in authoritative institutions • Content differs from that hosted in other Web sites • Lack of detailed information • Not supported by strong data or theories • Short papers • Messy structure • Documents appear in less prestigious sites only • Low usage • Small Web sites • Not recommended by experts • Documents received bad reviews

* *Note*: Data of American students are derived from Chapter 7.

The changing information environment and the increased reliance on information from the Internet by younger users require reassessment of the role of libraries. A study by the Pew Internet & American Life Project (2002) shows that 73% of college students report that they use the Internet more than the library, compared with only 9% who use the library more than the Internet for information searching. According to a recent study on the perceptions of libraries and information resources conducted by the OCLC (2005), respondents in the survey indicate that "search engines deliver better quantity and quality of information than librarian-assisted searching—and at greater speed." Librarians have traditionally served as gatekeepers, maintaining quality control on library materials. The habit of acquiring Web-based information by the younger generation highlights the need to educate them about how to conduct research, and educate the public about the value of library resources, not just those that are quick and easy. Kelley and Orr (2003) note that, "The lack of awareness of how much [information] is *not* available on the Web, and the seeming inability of students to understand why they should use library-supplied databases instead of Web-based sites, remains a significant pedagogical issue that our profession needs to address."

In the digital age, one of the new roles of librarians is to provide instructions and guidelines about how to assess Web-based information. Marcum (2003) points out that, "Librarians know the great value of curated print, but new generations of information seekers place higher value on convenience and speed than on carefully assembled and authoritative print collections." The arrival of the Internet presents unprecedented challenges, but not insurmountable ones. Libraries must continue to explore creative ways to deliver their services in the new information environment. Marcum (2003) proposes that one of the important research questions for the digital era library is, "Can library services be restructured to present high-quality, trusted information in digital form to meet the needs of users for truly useful material as well as for immediate, convenient access?"

Even though efforts were made to attract participants from diverse academic disciplines in this survey, it is very difficult to ensure a very balanced representation across all disciplines. Since students in different academic disciplines may have different attitudes toward the use of Web-based information for their studies, expansion of this chapter into exploring disciplinary differences in credibility assessment will be necessary to fully validate the findings.

This chapter is an extension of Chapter 7. It extends research on credibility perceptions by exploring how Chinese students make credibility assessments of Web-based information for their research, and what evaluation criteria they employ. As previously noted, credibility perception is deeply embedded in and heavily influenced by the social and cultural contexts. Cultural differences may have a significant impact on credibility assessment. Future research can extend the findings of this study by investigating similar research problems in different cultural contexts.

People in credibility assessment are active information seekers instead of passive information receivers. Stereotype-based expectations can affect people's attention to and interpretation of information based on the preexisting perceptions and images. This chapter explores credibility perceptions of documents hosted on a Web site in an advanced country by Chinese students. Another possible way of research might be to look at how people perceive information hosted in less developed countries in their credibility assessments.

In the digital environment, user expectations and patterns of library use are constantly evolving. It is crucial to find out to what extent they rely on Web-based information and to what extent they rely on library-provided resources.

The following chapter will investigate people's perceptions of and preferences for print and electronic resources. Circumstances that affect the selection of use between digital libraries and physical libraries will also be analyzed.

NOTES

1. Survey questions: The survey questions in this chapter are based on those in Chapter 7. A cluster of twenty questions (see Table 8.1) was used to measure the dimensions of credibility. Compared to face-to-face surveys, self-administered questionnaires have certain inherent limitations such as lower response rate and possible confusion about survey questions. A pilot project was conducted in December 2003. On the other hand, since most undergraduate and graduate students in China possess a good command of English, the questionnaire includes English and Chinese versions with the goal of achieving the greatest degree of consistency and comparability with Chapter 7.

2. How was the survey conducted? Two hundred copies of the questionnaire were distributed to students at Zhongshan University (Guangzhou, China) either in class, at student dormitories, or at the student center during the spring and summer of 2004. Participants in this study are undergraduate and graduate students from diverse disciplines such as business administration, computer science, economics, history, law, library and information science, mathematics, political science, and sociology. Participants were asked to fill out the questionnaire based on their experiences in selecting Web-based information for research purposes. One hundred and forty-five completed copies were returned: 74 copies from graduate students and 71 from undergraduate students. Survey results are shown in Table 8.1. The open-ended comments are grouped in ten categories and reported in Figure 8.1. The mean credibility ratings by undergraduate and graduate students are presented in Table 8.2.

REFERENCES

Burbules, N.C. (2001). Paradoxes of the Web: The Ethical Dimensions of Credibility. *Library Trends*, 49(3), 441–453.

Dong, X. (2003). Searching Information and Evaluation of Internet: A Chinese Academic Library User Survey. *International Information & Library Review*, 35(2–4), 163–187.

Fogg, B.J., Marshall, J., Laraki, O., Osipovich, A., Varma, C., Fang, N., Paul, J., Rangnekar, A., Shon, J., Swani, P., and Treinen, M. (2001). What Makes Web Sites Credible? In *Proceedings of ACM CHI 2001 Conference on Human Factors in Computing Systems* (pp. 61–68). New York, NY: ACM Press.

Friedlander, A. (2002). *Dimensions and Use of the Scholarly Information Environment*. Washington, DC: Digital Library Federation and Council on Library and Information Resources. Retrieved November 2, 2007, from http://www.clir.org/pubs/reports/pub110/contents.html.

Graham, L. and Metaxas, P.T. (2003). "Of Course It's True; I Saw It on the Internet!": Critical Thinking in the Internet Era. *Communications of the ACM*, 46(5), 70–75.

Grimes, D.J. and Boening, C.H. (2001). Worries with the Web: A Look at Student Use of Web Resources. *College & Research Libraries*, 62(1), 11–23.

Hamilton, D.L., Sherman, S.J., and Ruvolo, C.M. (1990). Stereotype-Based Expectancies: Effects on Information Processing and Social Behavior. *Journal of Social Issues*, 46(2), 35–60.

Herring, S.D. (2001). Using the World Wide Web for Research: Are Faculty Satisfied? *Journal of Academic Librarianship*, 27(3), 213–219.

Kandell, J.J. (1998). Internet Addition on Campus: The Vulnerability of College Students. *CyberPsychology & Behavior*, 1(1), 11–17.

Kelley, K.B. and Orr, G.J. (2003). Trends in Distant Student Use of Electronic Resources: A Survey. *College & Research Libraries*, 64(3), 176–191.

Marcum, D.B. (2003). Research Questions for the Digital Era Library. *Library Trends*, 51(4), 636–651.

Metzger, M.J., Flanagin, A.J., and Zwarun, L. (2003). College Student Web Use, Perceptions of Information Credibility, and Verification Behavior. *Computers & Education*, 41, 271–290.

OCLC White Paper on the Information Habits of College Students (2002). *How Academic Librarians Can Influence Students' Web-Based Information Choices*. Retrieved February 23, 2008, from http://www5.oclc.org/downloads/community/informationhabits.pdf.

OCLC (2005). *Perceptions of Library and Information Resources*. Dublin, OH: OCLC. Retrieved February 23, 2008, from http://www.oclc.org/reports/2005perceptions.htm.

Pew Internet & American Life Project (2002). *The Internet Goes to College: How Students Are Living in the Future With Today's Technology*. Retrieved March 23, 2007, from http://www.pewinternet.org/pdfs/PIP_College_Report.pdf.

Rieh, S.Y. (2002). Judgment of Information Quality and Cognitive Authority in the Web. *Journal of the American Society for Information Science and Technology*, 53(2), 145–161.

Scholz-Crane, A. (1998). Evaluating the Future: A Preliminary Study of the Process of How Undergraduate Students Evaluate Web Sources. *Reference Services Review*, 26(3–4), 53–60.

Stanford, J., Tauber, E., Fogg, B.J., and Marable, L. (2002). *Experts vs. Online Consumers: A Comparative Credibility Study of Health and Finance Web Sites*. Retrieved February 23, 2008, from http://www.consumerwebwatch.org/news/report3_credibilityresearch/slicedbread.pdf.

Tenopir, C. (2003). *Use and Users of Electronic Library Resources: An Overview and Analysis of Recent Research Studies*. Retrieved February 23, 2008, from http://www.clir.org/pubs/reports/pub120/pub120.pdf.

9

PRINT VERSUS ELECTRONIC RESOURCES: USER PERCEPTIONS, PREFERENCES, AND USE

The arrival and proliferation of electronic resources and digital libraries have already influenced and changed the way students and scholars use print resources and physical libraries. It has also sparked a new wave of literature on the perceptions and preferences of print and electronic resources. In a recent article, Tenopir (2003a) stresses the following questions that need to be answered in the coming decade, such as how does the information medium affect people's preferences and use? Do people use information delivered in digital formats differently from print formats? The increased reliance on electronic resources also requires reexamination of the changes in information seeking behaviors in the digital environment and their implications for library services (Marcum, 2003).

This chapter focuses on the extent to which graduate students in a metropolitan university setting use print and electronic resources. It also examines the importance of subject discipline to reading preferences and use of print and electronic resources. Circumstances affecting the choice between physical and digital libraries are also discussed. Studying these issues would enable us to better understand the changing patterns of information use in the increasingly intensive digital environment.

Over the past few years, people's perceptions of and preferences for print and electronic resources have been the focus of numerous studies. The intellectual ferment attending this dramatic development has brought with it a

---

This chapter is an updated and expanded version of an earlier article: Liu, Z. (2006). Print vs. electronic resources: A study of user perceptions, preferences, and use. *Information Processing and Management*, 42(2), 583–592.

wealth of new studies and approaches. It is not the purpose of this chapter to discuss these different studies. Nevertheless, an examination of related literature reveals that there are some essential studies that deserve closer attention.

Most of these studies were conducted in the academic environment, with particular attention given to surveying students and faculty. Dilevko and Gottlieb's (2002) web-based survey of undergraduate library users at the University of Toronto finds that, while undergraduate students typically begin assignments and essays using electronic resources, traditional print resources (e.g., books and printed journals) remain crucial components in their research because of their reliability and permanent accessibility.

Electronic formats have achieved a growing popularity, especially among younger users. A survey of college students by M. Rogers (2001) indicates that 62% of them prefer electronic formats over paper versions. Strouse (2004) shows that users (especially younger users) have developed a clear preference for receiving information in electronic formats. Liew, Foo, and Chennupati (2000) conduct a survey of eighty-three graduate students to study their use and perceptions of electronic journals. They find that a vast majority of graduate students (73%) prefer electronic journals over print journals. Commonly cited reasons include links to additional resources, searching capability, currency, availability, and ease of access. However, a recent study of students at the University of Hong Kong demonstrates that an overwhelming majority (77%) of the respondents still favor print over electronic materials. Old habits attached to print media, portability, and readability are the chief factors leading to the preference for print materials (Bodomo, Lam and Lee, 2003).

Studies have found that students and faculty exhibit marked differences in the perceptions of and preferences for print and electronic resources. Sathe, Grady, and Giuse (2002) report that fellows, students, and residents favor electronic journals, while faculty prefer print journals. Ease of access, ease of printing, and ease of searching are among the most commonly cited reasons for preferring electronic journals. On the other hand, respondents value the readability of print journals because they have better graphic quality and are easier to browse. In a survey of physicians' attitudes toward electronic journals, Wright and others (2001) find that 74% of the respondents in their survey raise concerns about losing the convenient readability and portability of print journals. Bonthron and other researchers (2003) examine the views of academic staff and students at the University of Edinburgh on the advantages and limitations of electronic journals. Their results indicate that "academic staff incorporate electronic journal usage into their working patterns in different ways than students and that these differences may affect attitudes toward support services (library Web pages, virtual learning environments) designed to promote electronic journal usage."

In an investigation of faculty electronic journal usage at the University of Georgia, Smith (2003) reports that junior faculty tend to use electronic resources more than senior faculty. Lenares (1999) finds that convenience, timeliness, and the ability to search text are the most important factors influencing faculty's choice of electronic over print materials. On the other hand, the ability to browse, portability, physical comfort, and convenience are the most important characteristics leading them to choose print over electronic resources. One significant asset of print journals is archiving and long-term access. A survey among faculty members at Texas A&M University indicates that a majority (55%) of the respondents prefer print versions. Primary reasons include dislike reading from a screen, difficulties in navigating electronic documents, and future access (Tenner and Yang, 1999).

Access to electronic resources not only influences the way students and scholars conduct research, it also changes the way they use the traditional resources. At Ohio State University, faculty usage of electronic journals increased by 17.7% during 1998 and 2000, while print use deceased by 8.7% (S. Rogers, 2001).

Users' expectations of libraries and their patterns of library usage are changing as they find more information readily available from the Web. Boyce and other researchers (2004) examine how electronic journals are changing the reading patterns of scholars over the past decade. Friedlander (2002) finds that "faculty and graduate students seem to expect a hybrid environment of print and electronic resources, while undergraduates seem more willing to live in a wholly online world." Dillon and Hahn (2002) find that 70% of the faculty at the University of Maryland want core journals in both print and electronic formats.

A report released by the Pew Internet & American Life Project (2002) finds that 73% of college students reported they use the Internet more than the library for research; however, only 9% said that they still gather information in the old-fashioned way. Even within the realm of electronic resources, most undergraduate students often favor full-text resources that require least effort. Gravitating to the easily available web-based resources raises a number of concerns among librarians. Schaffner (2001) observes that, "on several occasions, students have requested assistance in changing the focus of their research to a topic that could be searched using only electronic sources." The trend toward the exclusive use of electronic resources should be the cause for concern about the direction of scholarship, since a wealth of research material is not now—and may never be—available in electronic formats (Schaffner, 2001). If students are so heavily reliant on recent online resources, they may be missing the historical context that most books provide (Schevitz, 2002).

Unlike users in traditional libraries, digital library users are basically invisible to librarians. Early and continuous involvement from potential participants is a critical step to understanding users' expectations so as to serve their needs more effectively (Giersch et al., 2004). Ackerman (1994) stresses that "as we build the digital library, we need to be careful not to carelessly obliterate some of the important features of current libraries." He further points out that "the need for help in selecting material, the desirability of informal information, the ad-hoc and contextual nature of most information seeking, the personal enjoyability and community benefits from social interaction—all argue for the inclusion of some form of social interaction within the digital library." Pomerantz and Marchionini (2007) also argue that the role of the library as a space for social activities will become increasingly important in the digital environment.

In summary, undergraduate students, graduate students, and faculty have different perceptions and preferences in their choice of print and electronic resources. Previous studies have focused on the perceptions and preferences of print and electronic resources of undergraduate students and faculty. However, few studies have focused on graduate students exclusively. Moreover, very little is known about the circumstances that influence their choice of format of resources and the type of libraries (i.e., physical vs. digital) to satisfy their information needs. This chapter explores the extent to which graduate students in a metropolitan university setting use print and electronic resources. For the purpose of this study, electronic resources include both electronic-only resources and materials that are available both electronically and in print.

A cluster of thirteen questions was designed to gather information about the perceptions, preferences, and use of print and electronic resources of graduate students. At the most basic level, the questionnaire[1] was designed to find out the following:

- What type of information sources do you usually consult first?
- How often do you use online sources for your studies?
- How often do you use print sources for your studies?
- How often do you read online?
- How often do you print out electronic documents?
- If you find the information you need from digital libraries, will you still try to look for more information from traditional libraries?
- If you find the information you need from traditional libraries, will you still try to look for more information from digital libraries?

These basic questions were designed with the goal of achieving a high response rate. Moreover, in order to achieve a deeper understanding of their preferences and circumstances that affect their choice of format of resources and the type of libraries (i.e., traditional vs. digital), an optional section consisting of the following six questions was included at the end of the questionnaire in an effort to gather their open-ended thoughts related to their preferences and use:

- In your opinion, what are the three most significant advantages of digital libraries?
- In your opinion, what are the three most significant advantages of traditional libraries?
- From your experience, what are the three most significant barriers in using digital libraries?

- From your experience, what are the three most significant barriers in using traditional libraries?
- Under what circumstances do you prefer digital libraries to traditional libraries?
- Under what circumstances do you prefer traditional libraries to digital libraries?

TYPES OF INFORMATION SOURCES FIRST CONSULTED

When asked what type of information sources respondents usually consult first when completing their assignments and essays, 51.9% of all respondents turn first to library online information resources (e.g., e-journals) and 28.6% to the World Wide Web (WWW; see Table 9.1). It seems that the characteristics of electronic resources (i.e., convenient access and ease in searching) are the chief factors contributing to the selection of these two most frequently cited first choices. Only 15.8% of all respondents begin with library printed sources (e.g., printed books and journals) when completing their assignments and essays. Five participants cite personal collections as their first choice.

Undergraduate students tend to use the WWW as a primary information source, usually with little regard to the reliability of the information. Graham and Metaxas (2003) report that undergraduate students prefer to search the Internet first for school-related tasks. A recent report released by Online Computer Library Center (OCLC) (2005) reveals that over 80% of information searches begin with a search engine, and only 2% of college students start their searches on a library Web site. Survey results by the Electronic Publishing Initiative (EPIC) at Columbia University further indicate that undergraduate students tend to be more heavily reliant on the WWW, while graduate students are more likely to depend on library-provided online resources.

Unlike most undergraduate students who first consult the Internet, over half of all graduate students in this survey (51.9%) first turn to library online information resources (e.g., e-journals). Graduate students are heavy users of library electronic resources. This finding is also confirmed by other recent studies (Rudner, Miller-Whitehead and Gellmann, 2002; Tenopir, 2003b). Even though students prefer using electronic resources, there is a marked difference between undergraduates and graduates in their use of library online resources. Graduate students are more likely to use library databases than their undergraduate counterparts (Kelley and Orr, 2003). Friedlander (2002) explains that the subscription of electronic journals is less than 1% among respondents. The low level of subscription implies that faculty and graduate students rely on third party access, presumably the library.

Recent studies have shown the importance of subject discipline to source preferences (Dilevko and Gottlieb, 2002; Smith, 2003). Another recent study by Siebenberg, Galbraith, and Brady (2004) also suggests that users' migration from print to electronic resources is dependent on the subject area. Table 9.1 shows that graduate students in different disciplines have different preferences for information sources when they complete their assignments and essays. In library and information science (LIS), 71.4% of the respondents cite

Table 9.1
Types of Information Sources First Consulted

Type of information sources	Library and information science (n = 42)	Business (n = 33)	Computer science (n = 35)	Social sciences (n = 23)	Total (n = 133)
Library online resources	30 (71.4%)	14 (42.4%)	13 (37.1%)	12 (52.2%)	69 (51.9%)
Library printed books	3 (7.1%)	0 (0.0%)	4 (11.4%)	3 (13.0%)	10 (7.5%)
Library printed journals	4 (9.5%)	3 (9.0%)	1 (2.9%)	3 (13.0%)	11 (8.3%)
World Wide Web (WWW)	4 (9.5%)	16 (48.5%)	14 (40.0%)	4 (17.4%)	38 (28.6%)
Others	1 (2.4%)	0 (0.0%)	3 (8.6%)	1 (4.3%)	5 (3.8%)

Note: Percentage figures of this and other tables may not add to 100% because of rounding.

library online sources as the first stop for information, compared to 42.4% in business, 37.1% in computer science, and 52.2% in social sciences ($x^2 =$ 12.27, $p < 0.01$). On the other hand, students in business and computer science tend to first consult information sources from the WWW more heavily than those in LIS and in social sciences: 48.5% in business and 40.0% in computer science vs. 9.5% in LIS and 17.4% in social sciences ($x^2 = 13.86$, $p < 0.01$). These statistical tests indicate that subject disciplines do make a difference in their choice of information, and LIS students are unique in their choice of using library online resources (e.g., e-journals). Factors that may affect the strong preference for library online resources by students in LIS include familiarity, availability, and convenience. It is very likely that students in LIS are more knowledgeable about or familiar with library online sources than students in other fields. Another explanation is that research materials in LIS may not be as readily available from the WWW as those in business administration and computer science.

The significance of subject discipline to source preferences is further confirmed by a similar study. In a study of distance graduate students' use of information sources at Texas A&M University (TAMU), Liu and Yang (2004) find that field differences are significantly related to the selection of primary information sources. More specifically, students in humanities and social sciences (37%) are more likely to use TAMU libraries as their primary information source than students in sciences and engineering (25%) and those in business and economics (11.5%). In contrast, students in business and economics are more likely to rely on the WWW as their primary source than students in other majors (e.g., humanities and social sciences, and science and engineering).

FREQUENCY OF USING ELECTRONIC AND PRINT SOURCES

Electronic sources are more frequently used than print sources. Table 9.2 shows that 84.2% of all respondents use electronic sources "all the time" or "most of the time," compared to 54.2% who use printed sources "all the time" or "most of the time." The use of electronic and print resources varies among different disciplines. Students in computer science, business, and LIS more heavily use electronic sources than those in social sciences. 91.4% of the respondents in computer science, 90.9% in business, and 85.7% in LIS report that they use electronic sources "all the time" or "most of the time," compared to only 60.9% in social sciences. On the other hand, students in LIS and social sciences use print sources more frequently than those in computer science and business.

FREQUENCY OF READING ONLINE AND PRINTING OUT

According to Table 9.3, 33.8% of all participants in this survey "always" or "frequently" read online. More specifically, students in computer science

Table 9.2
Frequency of Using Electronic and Print Sources

Frequency	Library and information science (n = 42)		Business (n = 33)		Computer science (n = 35)		Social sciences (n = 23)		Total (n = 133)	
	Electronic	Printed	Electronic	Printed	Electronic	Printed	Electronic	Printed	Electronic	Printed
All the time	14 (33.3%)	6 (14.3%)	15 (45.5%)	1 (3.0%)	14 (40.0%)	2 (5.7%)	9 (39.1%)	4 (17.4%)	52 (39.1%)	13 (9.8%)
Most of the time	22 (52.4%)	27 (64.3%)	15 (45.5%)	10 (30.3%)	18 (51.4%)	9 (25.7%)	5 (21.7%)	13 (56.5%)	60 (45.1%)	59 (44.4%)
Sometimes	4 (9.5%)	9 (21.4%)	3 (9.1%)	19 (57.6%)	2 (5.7%)	22 (62.9%)	5 (21.7%)	6 (26.1%)	14 (10.5%)	56 (42.1%)
Rarely	2 (4.8%)	0 (0.0%)	0 (0.0%)	3 (9.1%)	1 (2.9%)	2 (5.7%)	4 (17.4%)	0 (0.0%)	7 (5.3%)	5 (3.8%)
Never	0 (0.0%)	0 (0.0%)	0 (0.0%)	0 (0.0)	0 (0.0%)	0 (0.0%)	0 (0.0%)	0 (0.0%)	0 (0.0%)	0 (0.0%)

Table 9.3
Frequency of Reading Online and Printing Out Electronic Documents

Frequency	Library and information science (n = 42)		Business (n = 33)		Computer science (n = 35)		Social sciences (n = 23)		Total (n = 133)	
	Read Online	Print Out	Read Online	Print Out	Read Online	Print Out	Read Online	Print Out	Read Online	Print Out
Always	2 (4.8%)	8 (19.0%)	4 (12.1%)	7 (21.2%)	4 (11.4%)	8 (22.9%)	2 (8.7%)	5 (21.7%)	12 (9.0%)	28 (21.1%)
Frequently	7 (16.7%)	26 (61.9%)	11 (33.3%)	20 (60.6%)	12 (34.3%)	20 (57.1%)	3 (13.0%)	13 (56.5%)	33 (24.8%)	79 (59.4%)
Sometimes	17 (40.5%)	8 (19.0%)	10 (30.3%)	6 (18.2%)	17 (48.6%)	6 (17.1%)	8 (34.8%)	5 (21.7%)	52 (39.1%)	25 (18.8%)
Rarely	16 (38.1%)	0 (0.0%)	8 (24.2%)	0 (0.0%)	2 (5.7%)	1 (2.9%)	10 (43.5%)	0 (0.0%)	36 (27.1%)	1 (0.8%)
Never	0 (0.0%)	0 (0.0%)	0 (0.0%)	0 (0.0%)	0 (0.0%)	0 (0.0%)	0 (0.0%)	0 (0.0%)	0 (0.0%)	0 (0.0%)

(45.7%) and business (45.5%) tend to read more frequently online than those in LIS (21.4%) and social sciences (21.7%).

Even though the use of electronic sources and online reading habits vary by discipline, the frequency of printing out electronic documents is surprisingly similar across all disciplines: 80.9% of the respondents in LIS, 81.8% in business, 80.0% in computer science, and 78.3% in social sciences report that they "always" or "frequently" print out electronic documents. This pattern is consistent with the findings in a number of recent studies. Respondents in other studies consistently report that they prefer printing out electronic documents for reading, and then do most of their reading from the printout (Cherry and Duff, 2002; King and Montgomery, 2002; McKnight, 1997). In the field of medicine, most users don't read journal articles on the computer screen and tend to print articles for reading (Sathe, Grady and Giuse, 2002). In a study of 1050 18–24-year-old U.S. college students who use the Internet for school-related assignments, an OCLC white paper (2002) also indicates that respondents repeatedly mentioned the need to print electronic resources. Reading a real book is different from reading on a computer screen. One respondent notes that while electronic resources bring enormous convenience when someone searches for something specific, print material is much more user-friendly. Reading print materials is less distracting than reading online. It seems that many people search or browse digital documents, but when they need to have an in-depth reading of a document, they prefer to print it out for annotation. Participants in another study also report that print documents not only facilitate annotations, but also enable easier comparisons to be made among all gathered sources (Dilevko and Gottlieb, 2002). Marshall (1997) notes that "support for a smooth integration of annotating with reading—is the most difficult to interpret from a design point of view; yet, it is potentially the most important." It is very likely that people will continue to print out electronic documents for annotation, even as they read materials in a digital library (Marshall, 1997).

NEED FOR A MIX OF PRINT AND ONLINE RESOURCES

Motivation seems to play an important role in the selection of information sources. Liu and Yang (2004) find that highly motivated users choose libraries as their primary information sources, whereas less-motivated users tend to heavily depend on the Internet and other resources. It seems that the motive for a comprehensive coverage of sources (i.e., print and digital) and for not missing something that is important is a chief factor for looking at additional information from different types of libraries.

In response to the question: "If you find the information you need from digital libraries, will you still try to look for more information from traditional libraries," 75.9% of all participants in this survey express the need to continue looking for more information from traditional libraries. Following are the

Table 9.4
The Need for Additional Information from Different Types of Libraries

	Will still look for more information from traditional libraries	Will still look for more information from digital libraries
Yes	101 (75.9%)	114 (85.7%)
No	32 (24.1%)	19 (14.3%)
Total	133 (100.0%)	133 (100.0%)

most commonly cited reasons for supplementing online resources with print resources: to confirm the information found in digital libraries; to find more information from books; to browse the bookshelves; to find quality and reliable sources; and to get older materials. One participant notes that, "Not all information is available electronically. I hate missing something that is really important." It seems that graduate students are concerned about the coverage and quality of information obtained from digital libraries. Although students may turn to online resources first, they still utilize print resources in physical libraries for various reasons. Generally speaking, current information is more heavily used than older information. But we should not forget that in the digital age where new information is widely available, people still need to use older materials (see Chapter 3). Tenopir and King (1998) note that it is likely that older materials are used for research purposes while new information is used for keeping up-to-date.

Nearly 25% of the participants indicate there is no need to supplement online resources with print resources. One participant points out: "If I have already found what I need, I will stop." Another participant indicates that "it will take too much time to find additional information" from traditional libraries. Similar findings are reported by EPIC at Columbia University. It finds that about 30% of the respondents admit that they don't go further than electronic resources, and about 20% of the respondents agree that "their widespread use of electronic resources is so pervasive that they have not learned how to use the physical library."

As shown in Table 9.4, over 85% of all participants report the need to supplement print resources with online resources. The need for current information, coverage of materials not published in print, and the desire to find complete sources are the primary reasons stated by participants. One respondent says: "I am hooked on digital. Digital libraries have good information as well." It is also interesting to note that a respondent indicates the desire to have documents in portable document format (pdf) in order to be able to print *clean* copies as the reason for looking to digital libraries for additional information. The need for full-text journal articles has been reported in a number of recent studies. A 2002 OCLC white paper indicates that most respondents use full-texts of journal articles during their most recent electronic visit of library resources.

Approximately 15% of all participants report no need to look for additional information from digital libraries. Following are the reasons for not needing to supplement print resources with online information: "I don't want to spend time in front of computers if I don't have to—I am on computers all day at work!," "Sometimes you get so much information. It is hard to see what you really need," and "When I expect to find the information in a traditional library, that is what I want."

The majority of participants in this survey desire to meet their information needs through a mix of print and online resources, even though their reasons for supplementing another type of information differ. Graduate students seem to expect a hybrid of print and electronic resources. This finding is further confirmed by a few recent studies (Dilevko and Gottlieb, 2002; Friedlander, 2002). Friedlander (2002) also argues that the desire for different media implies that the net effect of electronic sources is additive, and library use is changing rather than diminishing. The need for a hybrid of print and electronic resources implies that "digital collections are not going to be a substitute for existing and future library collections and plans must be made to accommodate both" (Kuny, 1997). It also suggests the need for librarians and faculty members to guide students to high quality information in electronic as well as print formats (Tenopir, 2003a). The desire for information from different types of libraries is also closely related to students' perceptions of digital as well as traditional libraries (see Tables 9.5 and 9.6).

PERCEIVED ADVANTAGES AND LIMITATIONS

A study by Melgoza, Mennel, and Gyeszly (2002) finds that most academic library users, whether faculty or students, rank accessibility as the most influential factor when they search for information, followed by convenience and ease of use. A recent study on user's expectations and suggestions of digital libraries (DLs) indicates that users rank "information should be found easily and quickly in DLs" and "being able to be easily familiarized with DLs" as the two most important requirements of digital libraries (Kani-Zabihi, Ghinea and Chen, 2006). Survey results presented in Table 9.5 and Table 9.6 further confirm these findings.

Electronic resources lend themselves to availability beyond time and location constraints. According to Table 9.5, digital libraries have a number of advantages that are absent from traditional libraries such as remote access, 24-hour access, and multiple users for a single source. Respondents report that the main advantages of digital libraries are that digital libraries allow them to get information outside the library, to obtain full-text journal articles in advance of the print version, and give them greater access with less effort. Remote and effortless access to full-text databases at midnight would epitomize the 24/7 mentality and convenience. French scientists also report similar findings in a study of the use of electronic journals. Mahé, Andrys, and Chartron

Table 9.5
Perceived Advantages of Digital and Traditional Libraries

Digital libraries	Traditional libraries
Accessibility (remote access; 24-hour access; quick access; wider access; earlier access). Availability (no need to worry about a source being checked out; no limit on what you can "take out"). Multiple use for single sources. Search capability. Links to additional information.	Physical browsing/being able to touch a real book. Getting immediate help from a "real" person. Quiet place for study/good atmosphere. Communal space for learning (e.g., public events and training programs). Getting more detailed information (e.g., books). Access to archival and older information.

(2000) find that direct access to the full text, no need to visit a library and make photocopies, no risks of needed articles being checked out or in the bindery, are among the most frequently cited advantages. Morse and Clint-worth (2000) report that there is overwhelming preference of users for electronic access, especially when they can link directly from databases to the full-text journal articles. In addition, respondents value the "links to additional information" because digital libraries offer users pathways to information via hyperlinks and one can easily maneuver through by a simple click from a comfortable chair rather than a time-consuming library visit.

However, physical libraries also have their unique advantages (e.g., physical browsing, getting immediate help from a real person, and communal space for learning). One respondent says: "I love the smell of old books." It seems that touching a print book is perceived as an advantage of a physical library. In a survey of 3234 students and faculty members at nearly 400 colleges and universities between late 2001 and early 2002, Greenstein and Healy (2002) find that print remains important. Over half of the respondents in their survey report that browsing library stacks or journals shelves remains an important way to obtain information.

The digital environment offers a number of new service opportunities such as virtual reference. But participants in this survey also indicate the importance of getting help from a "real" person, and they perceive impersonal services as a limitation in the digital environment (see also Table 9.6). Reference service is perhaps the most personal service offered by traditional libraries. People may feel that a "real" librarian at a traditional reference desk will better serve them than getting reference questions answered via e-mail from someone they cannot see. A 2002 OCLC white paper also indicates that students prefer face-to-face interaction over online or even telephone contact if they need help when using the Web for school-related assignments. Balas (2003) notes that "reference service doesn't mean settling for an impersonal service

Table 9.6
Perceived Barriers of Digital and Traditional Libraries

Digital libraries	Traditional libraries
Interface design problems (e.g., difficult to use).	Time consuming (e.g., travel time and parking).
Hard to ask for immediate help (e.g., lack of a "real" librarian; very impersonal).	Inconvenience (e.g., open hours; closed during holidays; check out and return materials).
Instability of online resources.	Availability (needed items have been checked out or not on the shelf).
Need equipment and Internet access (e.g., shift financial burden to users).	Easier to print at home than copy at libraries.
Discomfort with online reading.	
Credibility and quality issues.	Annoying patrons and unpleasant staff.
Technical problems (e.g., system malfunction; poor dial-up connection).	Library policy (e.g., short loan period; limited number of items to borrow; overdue fines; cannot have snacks and drinks).

that sacrifices quality for immediacy or 24/7 availability" and the "reference librarian is virtual *and* real."

In addition to traditional attachments and the desire for face-to-face interaction, physical libraries associated with them are seen as communal space for learning, quiet places for study with exhaustive new as well as archived information.

The ability to access information that is not available locally is cited as the most notable advantage of digital libraries. The most frequently cited barrier of a digital library is its difficulty to use (e.g., hard to do effective searches, hard to move back and forth between two things, and hard to return to a document if careful notes are not taken). One respondent also points out that it is difficult to find non-English information in digital libraries because of the problem in keying foreign characters. Instability of online resources is another major concern. One respondent states: "Sometimes I am worried that my online sources will disappear prior to completing my research paper."

CIRCUMSTANCES AFFECTING THE CHOICE BETWEEN DIGITAL LIBRARIES AND TRADITIONAL LIBRARIES

What type of libraries (i.e., traditional vs. digital) do respondents choose to satisfy their information needs?

In an information abundant environment where there are many alternatives to access free information, it is not surprising to find that few people are willing to pay a fee for information. A 2002 OCLC white paper reveals that 88% of the respondents completely agree that they are not likely to use a site that

Table 9.7
Circumstances Affecting the Use of Digital and Traditional Libraries

Preference for digital libraries over traditional libraries	Preference for traditional libraries over digital libraries
When I need to study all night (e.g., do research at 3 am).	When books are the primary sources of information.
When I don't want to travel (e.g., safer than being on the road).	When I need immediate help from a reference librarian.
When I need to get information quickly.	When I need to browse the collection.
When I need articles rather than books.	When I need a quiet place for study (e.g., get away from kids).
When doing preliminary research.	
When assignments require up-to-the-minute information or when brief assignments are of limited scope.	When I have to pay for online journals. When I need detailed and serious sources for major assignments. When I read something for pleasure.
When I need to use a printer (e.g., library photocopying is costly).	

charges a fee for accessing information. There is a trend that today's library users in increasing numbers are opting to print articles rather than photocopy from print issues (Morse and Clintworth, 2000).

As shown in Table 9.7, cost has a far-reaching effect on the selection of use between digital and physical libraries. When they need to use their printers to avoid costly photocopying at physical libraries, they will prefer to use digital libraries. It seems that making photocopies is a chore that most respondents strongly dislike and paying to photocopy print materials is a deterrent to their use. However, if respondents had to pay to use online journals, they would prefer using physical libraries. Sathe, Grady, and Giuse (2002) find that respondents "valued access from home and fast, free printing" rather than "locate and photocopy an article at a fee" in a physical library. Table 9.6 also shows that paying overdue fines is perceived as a drawback of traditional libraries.

Physical space is often a deciding factor for people to use traditional libraries when they want to browse the shelves, find a quiet place to study or discuss a group project, sit down to read something for pleasure, sign up for free training classes, and request hands-on help.

Twait's study (2005) shows that students rely on content relevance, familiarity, reputation/credibility, and convenience when making source selection decisions. Liu and Yang (2004) report that the least effort theory prevails in the users' selection and use of information sources. As shown in Table 9.7, the decision of use between digital and traditional libraries is situational. For example, users prefer using digital libraries when they need to do research at midnight, when they need to get information immediately, or when assignments require up-to-the-minute information. Dilevko and Gottlieb (2002) also find that undergraduate students prefer electronic resources over their print equivalents when they want to cut and paste quotations directly into their essays. However, when users need a quiet place for study (e.g., get away from kids), or when they require immediate help from a reference librarian, they will switch to a physical library.

It seems that seriousness of tasks also affects the students' choice between digital libraries and physical libraries. For small assignments or doing preliminary research, students are more likely to turn to the Internet and digital libraries. However, for major assignments that require detailed and serious sources or when books are the primary sources of information, they are more likely to use physical libraries since books provide good background information as well as thorough analyses of the subject.

CONCLUSION

Kuny (1997) states: "The importance of libraries has been diminished in the popular press as the pressures from industry encourage consumers to see libraries as anachronistic while the Internet and electronic products such as Microsoft Encarta are promoted as inevitable replacements." Even though people are very likely to continue to use electronic resources more frequently than print resources in the future, we must also keep in mind that users' purposes and preferences are very diverse and their source selection decisions are situational, and that there is not a single format that is ideal to all.

In a recent study of user's suggestions and expectations of digital libraries' functionality and features, Kani-Zabihi, Ghinea, and Chen (2006) find that "users were not too keen on reading e-books in DLs, but wished instead to see information about books being made available in DLs." Pomerantz and Marchionini (2007) argue that "digital libraries are not suitable replacements for physical libraries in all aspects of library functionality. Physical libraries will continue to evolve and thrive, often adding digital appendages that augment both functionality and community."

Users desire a hybrid information environment in which online information does not supplant information in print but adds new access opportunities for users to choose. Digital and traditional libraries have their unique advantages and limitations; they satisfy the information needs of users in different circumstances. Each plays a different role and serves the needs of users in different ways. Digital libraries offer a wide range of new access opportunities that are absent in the traditional environment, including remote access, 24-hour access, and multiple users for single sources. However, the desire for physical browsing, the need for immediate help from a "real" person, and the desire for communal space for learning—make a case for the importance of the traditional service environment. The hybrid library is likely to be a model for the foreseeable future (Brophy, 2001; Leggate, 1998; Pinfield, 1998). Grafton

(2007) states: "For now and for the foreseeable future, any serious reader will have to know how to travel down two very different roads simultaneously. No one should avoid the broad, smooth, and open road that leads through the screen. . . . But these streams of data, rich as they are, will illuminate, rather than eliminate, books and prints and manuscripts that only the library can put in front of you. The narrow path still leads, as it must, to crowded public rooms where the sunlight gleams on varnished tables, and knowledge is embodied in millions of dusty, crumbling, smelly, irreplaceable documents and books."

A recent Pew Internet and American Life Project Study (2002) reports that 80% of respondents turn first to free search engines for research, and only 6% choose online libraries. One of the librarian's important roles and responsibilities is to educate the public about the value of library's print and online resources. Faster and easier is not always better. Librarians and faculty members can work together to connect students to library resources.

The transition from print to digital environment adds "a layer of users we do not know—and probably never will," therefore, user studies "become increasingly important as libraries move from housing materials to providing electronic access to them" (Marcum, 2003). Librarians face a new challenge in reaching invisible users who have only electronic access to libraries. The increased reliance on electronic resources also requires reexamination of whom we serve. Buckland (2003) observes that all digital libraries have been designed backwards because "library services should be user-centered rather than data-centered". He further notes: "Only when substantially more research and development has been completed from the library user's perspective can the digital library environment begin to have the look and feel to good library service." We need to understand what patterns are emerging in the digital environment so that we can plan effective and responsive services.

This chapter focuses on the extent to which graduate students in a metropolitan university setting use print and electronic resources. The geographical limitations and small sample size of this study mean that the results cannot be generalized across all academic institutions. Many respondents in this survey are distance learners, which may in turn affect their preferences for and use of print and electronic resources. Studies in other geographical regions are needed to fully validate the findings.

It should also be noted that an entire generation is growing up with new technology and is likely to have different expectations and preferences toward the choice of digital and physical libraries. For example, many people like the smell of print books. However, it is unclear that this traditional attachment will continue to extend to the younger generation who naturally gravitate to the generally available Web tools (e.g., search engines), but are less familiar with physical libraries. Future studies are needed to continually monitor the changes in people's perceptions and preferences, and their resultant impact on the selection of use between digital and physical libraries.

NOTES

1. How was the survey conducted? One hundred and eighty copies of the questionnaire were distributed to students at San Jose State University either in class, at the library, or at the student center during the spring 2004 semester. Therefore, this is a sample of convenience rather than a random sample. Participants in this study are graduate students from diverse disciplines. They were asked to fill out the questionnaires based on their experiences in using electronic and print resources for research purposes and to complete the optional open-ended questions, if possible. Of the 136 questionnaires returned, 133 are complete and 3 incomplete. Among the 133 completed questionnaires, 42 are from students in library and information science (LIS), 33 from business administration, 35 from computer science, and 23 from social sciences (e.g., history and political science). The results of the 133 completed questionnaires are presented in Tables 9.1–9.4. Fifty-one of the 133 completed questionnaires include answers to the optional section. Results from the 51 individuals who completed the optional questions are summarized in Tables 9.5–9.7.

REFERENCES

Ackerman, M.S. (1994). Providing Social Interaction in the Digital Libraries. In *Proceedings of Digital Libraries 1994: First Annual Conferences on the Theory and Practice of Digital Libraries* (pp.198–200). Retrieved February 24, 2008, from http://www.csdl.tamu.edu/DL94/position/ackerman.html.

Balas, J.L. (2003). Is the Reference Librarian Real or Virtual? *Computers in Libraries*, 23, 48–51.

Bodomo, A., Lam, M., and Lee, C. (2003). Some Students Still Read Books in the 21st Century: A Study of User Preferences for Print and Electronic Libraries. *The Reading Matrix*, 3(3), 34–49. Retrieved November 2, 2007, from http://www.readingmatrix.com/articles/bodomo_lam_lee/article.pdf.

Bonthron, K., Urquhart, C., Thomas, R., Armstrong, C., Ellis, D., Everitt, J., Fenton, R., Lansdale, R., McDermott, E., Morris, H., Phillips, R., Spink, S., and Yeoman, A. (2003). Trends in Use of Electronic Journals in Higher Education in the UK—Views of Academic Staff and Students. *D-Lib Magazine*, 9(6). Retrieved November 2, 2007, from http://www.dlib.org/dlib/june03/urquhart/06urquhart.html.

Boyce, P., King, D.W., Montgomery, C., and Tenopir, C. (2004). How Electronic Journals Are Changing Patterns of Use. *The Serials Librarian*, 46(1–2), 121–141.

Brophy, P. (2001). *The Library in the Twenty-First Century: New Services for the Information Age*. London, England: Library Association Publishing.

Buckland, M.K. (2003). Five Grand Challenges for Library Research. *Library Trend*, 51(4), 675–686.

Cherry, J.M. and Duff, W.M. (2002). Studying Digital Library Users Over Time: A Follow-Up *Survey of* Early Canadiana Online. *Information Research*, 7(2).

Retrieved November 6, 2007, from http://informationr.net/ir/7-2/ paper123.html.

Dilevko, J. and Gottlieb, L. (2002). Print Sources in an Electronic Age: A Vital Part of the Research Process for Undergraduate Students. *Journal of Academic Librarianship*, 28(6), 381–392.

Dillon, I.F. and Hahn, K.L. (2002). Are Researchers Ready for the Electronic-Only Journal Collection? *Portal: Libraries and Academy*, 2(3), 375–390. *The Electronic Publishing Initiative at Columbia (EPIC) Online Survey of College Students: Executive Summary.* Retrieved November 6, 2007, from http://epic.columbia.edu/eval/find09/find09.html.

Friedlander, A. (2002). *Dimensions and Use of the Scholarly Information Environment.* Washington, DC: Digital Library Federation and Council on Library and Information Resources. Retrieved November 2, 2007, from http://www.clir.org/pubs/reports/pub110/contents.html.

Giersch, S., Klotz, E.A., McMartin, F., Muramatsu, B., Renninger, K.A., Shumar, W., and Weimar, S.A. (2004). If You Build It, Will They Come? Participant Involvement in Digital Libraries. *D-Lib Magazine*, 10(7–8). Retrieved November 2, 2007, from http://www.dlib.org/dlib/july04/giersch/07giersch.html.

Grafton, A. (2007, November 5). Future Reading: Digitization and Its Discontents. *New Yorker*, 83(34). Retrieved November 20, 2007, from http://www.newyorker.com/reporting/2007/11/05/071105fa_fact_grafton.

Graham, L. and Metaxas, P.T. (2003). "Of Course It's True; I Saw It on the Internet!" Critical Thinking in the Internet Era. *Communications of the ACM*, 46(5), 70–75.

Greenstein, D. and Healy, L.W. (2002). Print and Electronic Information: Shedding New Light on Campus Use. *Educause Review*, 37(5), 16–17. Retrieved November 6, 2007, from http://www.educause.edu/ir/library/pdf/erm02511.pdf.

Kani-Zabihi, E., Ghinea, G., and Chen, S.Y. (2006). Digital Libraries: What Do Users Want? *Online Information Review*, 30(4), 395–412.

Kelley, K.B. and Orr, G.J. (2003). Trends in Distant Student Use of Electronic Resources: A Survey. *College & Research Libraries*, 64(3), 176–191.

King, K.W. and Montgomery, C.H. (2002). After Migration to an Electronic Journal Collection: Impact on Faculty and Doctoral Students. *D-Lib Magazine*, 8(12). Retrieved November 6, 2007, from http://www.dlib.org/dlib/december02/king/12king.html.

Kuny, T. (1997). The Digital Dark Ages? Challenges in the Preservation of Electronic Information. 63rd IFLA Council and General Conference. Retrieved November 9, 2007, from http://www.ifla.org/IV/ifla63/63kuny1.pdf.

Leggate, P. (1998). Acquiring Electronic Products in the Hybrid Library: Prices, Licenses, Platforms And Users. *Serials*, 11 (2), 103–108.

Lenares, D. (1999). Faculty Use of Electronic Journals at Research Institutions. In *Proceedings of the 9th National Conference of the Association of College & Research Libraries*. Retrieved November 6, 2007, from http://www.ala.org/ala/acrl/acrlevents/lenares99.pdf.

Liew, C.L., Foo, S., and Chennupati, K.R. (2000). A Study of Graduate Student End-Users; Use and Perception of Electronic Journals. *Online Information Review*, 24(4), 302–315.

Liu, Z. and Yang, Z. (2004). Factors Influencing Distance-Education Graduate Students' Use Of Information Sources: A User Study. *Journal of Academic Librarianship*, 30(1), 24–35.

Mahé, A., Andrys, C., and Chartron, G. (2000). How French Research Scientists Are Making Use of Electronic Journals: A Case Study Conducted at Pierre et Marie Curie University and Denis Diderot University. *Journal of Information Science*, 26(5), 291–302.

Marcum, D.B. (2003). Research Questions for the Digital Era Library. *Library Trends*, 51(4), 636–651.

Marshall, C.C. (1997). Annotation: From Paper Books to the Digital Library. In *Proceedings of the 2nd ACM International Conference on Digital Libraries* (pp.131–140). New York, NY: ACM Press.

McKnight, C. (1997). Electronic Journals: What Do Users Think of Them? In *Proceedings of International Symposium on Research, Development and Practice in Digital Libraries*. Tsukuba, Japan. Retrieved June 23, 2008, from http://www.dl.slis.tsukuba.ac.jp/ISDL97/proceedings/mcknight.html.

Melgoza, P., Mennel, P.A., and Gyeszly, S.D. (2002). Information Overload. *Collection Building*, 21(1), 32–43.

Morse, D.H. and Clintworth, W.A. (2000). Comparing Patterns of Print and Electronic Journal Use in an Academic Health Science Library. *Issues in Science and Technology Librarianship*, 28. Retrieved November 6, 2007, from http://www.library.ucsb.edu/istl/00-fall/refereed.html.

OCLC (2005). *Perceptions of Library and Information Resources*. Dublin, OH: OCLC. Retrieved November 6, 2007, from http://www.oclc.org/reports/2005perceptions.htm.

OCLC White Paper on the Information Habits of College Students (2002). *How Academic Librarians Can Influence Students' Web-Based Information Choices*. Retrieved November 1, 2007, from http://www5.oclc.org/downloads/community/informationhabits.pdf.

Pew Internet & American Life Project (2002). *The Internet Goes to College: How Students Are Living in the Future with Today's Technology*. Retrieved November 6, 2007, from http://www.pewinternet.org/pdfs/PIP_College_Report.pdf.

Pinfield, S. (1998). Managing the Hybrid Library. *SCONUL Newsletter*, 14, 41–44.

Pomerantz, J. and Marchionini, G. (2007). The Digital Library as Place. *Journal of Documentation*, 63(4), 505–533.

Rogers, M. (2001). Survey Reveals College Students' Growing Preference for E-Text. *Library Journal*, 126(2), 31.

Rogers, S. (2001). Electronic Journal Usage at Ohio State University. *College & Research Libraries*, 62(1), 25–34.

Rudner, L.M., Miller-Whitehead, M., and Gellmann, J.S. (2002). Who Is Reading On-Line Education Journals? Why? And What Are They Reading? *D-Lib Magazine*, 8(12). Retrieved November 6, 2007, from http://www.dlib.org/dlib/december02/rudner/12rudner.html.

Sathe, N.A., Grady, J.L., and Giuse, N.B. (2002). Print versus Electronic Journals: A Preliminary Investigation into the Effect of Journal Format on Research Processes. *Journal of the Medical Library Association*, 90(2), 235–243.

Schaffner, B.L. (2001). Electronic Resources: A Wolf in Sheep's Clothing. *College & Research Libraries*, 62(3), 239–249.

Schevitz, T. (2002, February 10). A New Chapter for Libraries: Preference for Online Research Has Its Price. *San Francisco Chronicle*. A-1.

Siebenberg, T.R., Galbraith, B., and Brady, E.E. (2004). Print versus Electronic Journal Use in Three Sci/Tech Disciplines: What's Going On Here? *College & Research Libraries*, 65(5), 427–438.

Smith, E.T. (2003). Changes in Faculty Reading Behaviors: The Impact Electronic Journals on the University of Georgia. *Journal of Academic Librarianship*, 29(3), 162–168.

Strouse, R. (2004). The Changing Face of Content Users and the Impact on Information Providers. *Online*, 28(5), 27–31.

Tenner, E. and Yang, Z. (1999). End-User Acceptance of Electronic Journals: A Case Study from a Major Academic Research Library. *Technical Services Quarterly*, 17(2), 1–14.

Tenopir, C. (2003a). Electronic Publishing: Research Issues for Academic Librarians and Users. *Library Trends*, 51(4), 614–635.

Tenopir, C. (2003b). *Use and Users of Electronic Library Resources: An Overview and Analysis of Recent Research Studies*. Retrieved November 26, 2007, from http://www.clir.org/pubs/reports/pub120/pub120.pdf.

Tenopir, C. and King, D.W. (1998). Designing Electronic Journals with 30 Yea0rs of Lessons from Print. *Journal of Electronic Publishing*, 4(2). Retrieved November 6, 2007, from http://www.press.umich.edu/jep/04-02/.

Twait, M. (2005). Undergraduate Students' Source Selection Criteria: A Qualitative Study. *Journal of Academic Librarianship*, 31(6), 567–573.

Wright, S.M., Tseng, W.T., and Kolodner, K. (2001). Physician Opinion About Electronic Publications. *American Journal of Medicine*, 110(5), 373–377.

10

—•·≡·•—

THE FUTURE OF PAPER IN THE
DIGITAL AGE

"I believe that the motion picture is destined to revolutionize our educational system and that in a few years it will supplant largely, if not entirely, the use of textbooks."

—Thomas Edison, 1922 (quoted in Cuban, 1986, p. 9)

What happens to paper in the digital era? Where is the paperless office? We have seen that many predictions about the impact of new information technologies go wrong, primarily because people have a high expectation of technologies while underestimating the "social-material complex," of which technologies are only a part (Williams, 1974). Meanwhile, there appear a number of unanticipated problems attending the new technologies, most of which involve social, cultural, organizational, and human factors.

Thomas Edison's vision of the educational revolution is merely one of many unfulfilled promises of technological change. Similar grand claims were made for paper. This chapter first examines trends in paper consumption, and then seeks to explain some of the primary reasons why people still stick with paper in the digital age.

THE FALLACY OF THE "PAPERLESS OFFICE"

The predictions of a paperless society have been around for decades. The term "paperless clearing houses" was probably first coined in 1966, when

This chapter draws in part from an earlier article: Liu, Z. and Stork, D. (2000). Is Paperless Really More? Rethinking the Role of Paper in the Digital Age. *Communications of the ACM*, 43(11), 94–97.

Harvard Business Review published a visionary article entitled "Data systems that cross company boundaries" by Kaufman (1966). But "paperlessness" did not enter the public attention until 1975, when a *Business Week* article, "The Office of the Future," made a series of predictions (Bradley, 2005).

Over the past thirty years, the paperless office attained exceptional popularity amid the speculation about what the office-of-the-future may look like. Experts have regularly predicted the advent of the paperless office as an inevitable result of technological advances. Fascination with purely technological solutions results in the premature conclusion that the future office would be fully electronic and without paper. Ironically, it is the newer and better technological innovations that have made the paperless office an unrealized dream. People use computers to create and revise documents. However, they ultimately print them out on paper. As the growth in the consumption of paper used by printing and writing over the past thirty years indicates, the paperless office seems even more distant now than when it was proposed. According to the American Forest & Paper Association (2006), the consumption of paper and paperboard per capita in the United States rose from 501 pounds in 1975 to 666 pounds in 2005. Paper consumption for printing and writing in the United States climbed from 16.4 million tons in 1983 to 23.4 million tons in 1993, and to 26.3 million tons in 2003. As shown in Table 10.1, shipments of uncoated sheet papers, which make up the largest proportion of office paper, remain fairly stable in the networked environment. It should be noted here that there are many factors affecting the consumption of office paper such as economic growth, employment trend, generational difference, and structural changes in the use of office paper. The recent slowdown in paper sales does not signal the arrival of the paperless office in the foreseeable future (Bradley, 2005).

The quest for the paperless office remains an unrealized dream in Canada as well. Today, we are still barraged by heavy streams of paper. A recent report by Statistics Canada smashes the myth of the paperless office, finding instead that paper consumption for printing and writing has doubled over twenty years from 1.2 million tons in 1983 to 2.9 million tons in 2003, even as Canadians adopt new technologies that are supposed to make paper obsolete. The consumption of paper for printing and writing per capita rose by 93.6% to 91.4 kilograms from the years 1983 to 2003—about 20,000 pages per person per year. The report states that "Not only is the notion of a paperless society defeated by existing data, but a visit to any modern office workplace will confirm that printers everywhere continue to spit out massive amounts of paper, and paper recycling bins are full." Offices today are still stuffed full of paper, and "the paperless office is the office that never happened" (Sciadas, 2006).

Table 10.2 shows that Japan's domestic demand for printing and communication paper grew steadily over the past ten years. According to the *Outlook for Domestic Demand for Paper and Paperboard in 2007* published

Table 10.1
Shipments of Uncoated Free Sheet
Papers in the United States

Year	Consumption (in thousands of tons)
1991	11,504
1992	12,170
1993	12,355
1994	13,304
1995	12,997
1996	13,165
1997	13,681
1998	13,605
1999	14,038
2000	13,898
2001	12,649
2002	12,428
2003	12,262
2004	12,555
2005	12,016

Source: American Forest & Paper Association, 2006.

Table 10.2
Japan's Domestic Demand for Printing and Communication Paper

Year	Consumption (in thousands of tons)
1996	10,727
1997	11,037
1998	10,868
1999	11,479
2000	11,864
2001	11,659
2002	11,473
2003	11,670
2004	11,982
2005	11,978
2006	12,012
2007	12,066

Source: Japan Paper Association. Available at: http://www.jpa.gr.jp/en/about/sta/index.html.

by the Japan Paper Association, printing and communication paper, which represents approximately 60% of the total paper demand in Japan, inched up by 0.3 to 11.99 million tons, hitting a record high for the first time in two years (2004 and 2005). It forecasts the domestic demand for printing and communication paper will increase by 0.4% to 12.07 million tons.

Many technological innovations have been developed to free us from the "burden" of paper, yet the consumption of paper continues to increase. Increased consumption is not confined to developed countries (e.g., United States, Canada, and Japan). Worldwide consumption of paper also more than doubled over the last two decades, especially in emerging Asian economies such as China (Sciadas, 2006). The growing consumption of paper in the office has highlighted the need, if not for a paperless office, then at least for a less-paper office. It is not difficult to see that professionals in today's business world are faced with the growing problems of managing the vast number of paper documents that flow into their office daily. The challenge is not to eliminate paper, but to manage it. With the increasing volume of printed information, retrieval becomes more difficult. Business professionals spend about 60% of their time on document handling (Warnock, 1991). A survey of information mismanagement in U.S. corporations reveals that large organizations lose one paper document every twelve seconds; 3% of all paper documents are incorrectly filed; 7.5% of paper documents are lost forever; disorganization in the workplace may cost executives up to six weeks of time per year; and the average executive spends three hours per week hunting for mislabeled, misfiled, or lost documents (Adams, 1995).

WILL PAPER DISAPPEAR IN THE DIGITAL AGE?

It is generally believed that the burgeoning of digital devices will affect the use and role of paper in the digital age. What the future of paper will be is one of the major concerns as we embark on the digital era. We tried to approach this issue not only by looking at trend analyses, but also by examining people's behaviors with paper and digital documents (e.g., reading). We found that there are a number of reasons why people still stick with paper in the digital world.

Print for Reading

Reading is closely related to annotating. Olsen (1994) finds that 63% of those interviewed preferred to annotate or underline articles as they read them. Griffiths and King (1993) find that 33% photocopied their personal subscriptions and 56% photocopied library collections in order to annotate and/or highlight the printed document. These findings strongly indicate that annotating documents is closely related to reading, especially in-depth reading. Electronic note taking is certainly possible, but it requires skills

Table 10.3
Shipments of Paper for File Folders and
Form Bond in the United States (in
thousands of tons)

Year	File folder	Form bond
1991	214	2,111
1992	244	2,079
1993	254	1,903
1994	277	2,044
1995	291	1,710
1996	286	1,747
1997	313	1,688
1998	298	1,594
1999	310	1,567
2000	333	1,378
2001	318	1,248
2002	324	1,204
2003	308	1,127
2004	337	1,103
2005	299	1,041

Source: American Forest & Paper Association, 2006.

greater than the use of a pencil or highlighter. This is one of the major reasons why people print for reading and annotating. Findings in Chapter 5 further indicate that readers will continue to use print media for much of their reading activities, especially for in-depth reading, since it usually involves annotating and highlighting. In the digital age, printing for reading remains one of the major driving forces for the increasing consumption of paper (Hart and Liu, 2003; Sellen and Harper, 2002).

People know how to organize and manipulate paper documents, but manipulating electronic documents requires a different set of skills. The long-standing practice of maintaining file folders of printed materials, arranged by topic, remains popular in the digital age. Table 10.3 indicates the growing consumption of paper for manufacturing file folders per capita in the United States, another indication of the growing use of printed information.

Behavior has a uniform pattern: scholars photocopy important articles, annotate and underline articles, and maintain a file of articles arranged most often by topics (Olsen, 1994). Sellen and Harper (2002) find people read across multiple documents as often as they read one document at a time. Spreading out multiple documents when reading and writing suggests the need of printing, since the computer screen cannot display conveniently many documents at the same time. Paper is the medium of choice for most reading activities, even when the high-tech devices are at hand (Sellen and Harper,

2002). People tend to feel more comfortable reading short documents rather than lengthy documents on the glowing screen; lengthy documents are more likely to be printed out (McKnight, 1997). This is another reason why people print for reading. Electronic documents can be conveniently used for browsing. However, in-depth reading activity is usually associated with writing and annotating. Findings in Chapter 6 demonstrate that digital and print media have their unique advantages and limitations. Each plays a different role and each serves the needs of users in different circumstances (see Table 6.7).

Credibility of Tangible Document Medium

The simple tangibility of the printed document is another reason for its continued popularity, despite the existence of electronic equivalents. People are generally comfortable with information only when they can "feel it" in their hands and can make sure whether the important information is recorded properly. Why are all the important messages and agreements (e.g., diplomas, certificates, and contracts) put on paper? One reason is that paper documents embrace credibility of information. The saying "put it on paper" conveys the importance of this tangible document medium. For example, an important document sent by e-mail, such as a job offer letter, is usually accompanied by a printed document via the post office. The fact that consumers give greater credence to what is in print than what is stated orally also exemplifies the feature of credibility of paper-based documents.

The general public perception of documents can be gleaned from dictionary definitions and from common use. According to *The American Heritage Dictionary of the English Language*, a document is a "written or printed paper bearing the original, official, or legal form of something, and which can be used to furnish decisive evidence or information." Heavily influenced by people's conventional perception of paper documents as evidence, important records (such as legal documents) are less likely to be transferred and preserved in digital forms only. The greater the importance of the message and higher the stakes, the more likely a person wants that message on paper. Problems (e.g., hackers, disaster recovery, and hard disk crash) also drive organizations to keep hard copies. The use of paper used for printing and copying is heavily influenced by business activities. According to Giga Information Inc., an average of 8.8 million sheets are used by a company per $100 million increase in revenue. File cabinets are used to store important printed records. According to BIFMA (Business and Institutional Furniture Manufacture's Association), the percentage of file cabinets in relation to other types of office furniture, like seating, desks, and tables, remains fairly stable over the past fifteen years (see Table 10.4).

As indicated in Chapter 4, many people today still have low confidence and trust in digital preservation. For example, few people today would throw away paper copies of important documents even if they have digital versions

Table 10.4
**Annual U.S. Production: Percentage
of File Cabinets in Relation to Other
Types of Office Furniture**

Year	Percentage
1990	15.1
1991	14.9
1992	15.1
1993	15.8
1994	14.3
1995	15.1
1996	13.8
1997	13.5
1998	12.8
1999	12.9
2000	12.4
2001	12.6
2002	13.1
2003	13.5
2004	14.1
2005	14.3
2006	13.3

Source: The Business and Institutional Furniture Manufacture's Association (BIFMA).
Available at: http://www.bifma.org/statistics/
index.html.

of exactly the same information. Fewer still would scan their paper documents
into a digital storage system and then throw away the paper. Paper documents
embrace credibility of information. Paper use is deeply rooted in our culture
and has had a profound impact on the civilization of our society. When one
considers replacing paper documents with electronic media, one should not
forget the historical root of paper documents. Electronic documents are being
gradually accepted as evidence, but we should remember that old habits die
hard. Whether electronic documents can replace paper documents as evidence
largely depends on the social acceptance of electronic documents as evidence.
Strassmann (1985) notes that paper-based documents will survive as long as
institutions deeply rooted in the vestiges of agricultural society continue to
operate. We will continue to use paper for some of the critical activities.

Paper Remains a Better Technology in Many Circumstances

In the digital environment, people use paper because of its advantages
rather than disadvantages. For example, people frequently print out directions

and maps from the Web because of the portability of paper documents. Sellen and Harper (2002) find that in the networked environment where it is very convenient to distribute documents electronically, people still want to distribute important documents in person, because delivering important documents in person enables people the opportunity to develop a smooth relationship and to make sure the important documents are there. Every time a student sends an assignment to me by e-mail, I always need to send a confirmation—I got it. If I don't do so within one or two days, I would receive e-mail messages from panicked students: "Have you received my assignment?"

About a decade ago, Hsu and Mitchell (1997) observed that a marketing professor at Stanford University utilized the school's first online business study case. The idea was to allow more efficient learning through the use of pictures and hypertext links. However, over 70% of the students in the class raised their hands when the professor asked: "How many of you printed the entire case rather than read it on the screen?"

Ten years later, a similar situation happened when I asked students in my classes, "How many of you printed out your online readings? How many of you read them online?" And this is on a campus in the heart of Silicon Valley, which does everything on computers and email! Students attending the library and information science program at San Jose State University may come to class with their slim laptops, where they may have the option to bring the required readings on their laptop and read the articles from the screen. However, the majority of students printed out their online readings and brought them to class. Why? One student pointed out—because it is easier to read on printed pages, and it is easier to underline key phrases and write notes with a pen in the margin, than to make notes on the laptop screen. On a computer, students would have to copy and paste the article in a word document, and somehow type in parentheses of notes here and there, which can be a hassle. Bolter (1991) notes: "No one technology of writing has ever proven adequate for all needs [and all situations]. The economy of writing is always diversified, as secondary technologies occupy places around the dominant one. These secondary technologies may even have been dominant ones that were pushed aside. Secondary technologies survive by meeting some need better than the dominant technology. The wax tablet remained in use from ancient times through the Middle ages, because it was convenient for rough drafts and other ephemera. . . . Stone has served as a medium for thousands of years when the writer wants a permanent, public display." Not a single type of document has ever proven adequate for all needs and ideal in all situations. New technologies do not necessarily displace the older ones. For example, it was once thought that microfilm would revolutionize printed media and lead to the end of the book. Microfilm remains, however, an important storage technology that has never seriously challenged the dominance of print. The advances in information technologies have not yet resulted in a paperless office that many people enthusiastically predicted in the 1970s.

While we are facing the transition to the paperless society, paper remains a better technology in many circumstances. For example, people's preference for paper as a medium of reading (especially in-depth reading) implies that paper is unlikely to disappear in the digital age. It is very likely that people will continue to print out electronic documents for annotation, even as they read materials in a digital library (Marshall, 1997; see Chapters 6 and 7 for more discussion).

New Technologies Do Not Always Replace Old Ones

New technologies are commonly misperceived as total replacements for old ones. For example, people may think of e-mail the same way they think of fax and postal mail. Far from rendering old technologies obsolete, the introduction of new technologies has often stimulated dynamic interactions between old and new technologies. Sometimes, the introduction of new technologies sparks new interest in old ones. For example, the invention of the printing press should have sounded the death knell for hand-written works, yet for several centuries quite the opposite occurred: "At the end of the fifteenth century, even though printing was by then well established, care for the elegant hand had not died out, and some of the most memorable examples of calligraphy still lay in the future. While books were becoming more easily available and more people were learning to read, more were also learning to write, often stylishly and with great distinction, and the sixteenth century became not only the age of the printed word but also the century of the great manuals of handwriting. It is interesting to note how often a technological development—such as Gutenberg's—promotes rather than eliminates that which it is supposed to supersede, making us aware of old-fashioned virtues we might otherwise have either overlooked or dismissed as of negligible importance" (Manguel, 1996).

Ample historical analogies exist regarding the impact of digital revolution on paper consumption. For example, the growth of the Web stimulates the growing use of paper by printers. The Internet and its seemingly boundless information sites have led to an increase in pages printed at home as well as in the office, with ever higher numbers of pages being printed closer to the end user. With an increasing amount of information available on the Web, more information is likely to be printed out. Also, as more people are reading online, more information is likely to be printed out. For instance, 63% of users printed documents from a Web browser in 1999, compared to about 8% in 1995 (Rivera, 2000). Information on the Web is ephemeral. If a user does not print out or store the documents immediately, he or she will run the risk of missing the needed information at a future date. This fear leads people to print out the information for their records.

Studies reveal that the use of e-mail also contributes to the growing use of paper by printers. While the use of e-mail for distributing documents has reduced the role of paper for the delivery itself, it has not done away with paper together. Many e-mail messages and attachments tend to be printed out. According to International Data Corporation, the introduction of e-mail into an organization caused up to a 40% increase in paper consumption. A recent study by Ivey Business Consulting for Lexmark (April 2003) finds that business documents represent 62% of pages being printed, while e-mail and the Internet account for averages of 16% and 9% of total print volumes, respectively.

Electronic media and printed media tend to complement and, in some ways, even reinforce each other. Today, paper remains popular because of its credibility, ease of use, portability, and its compatibility with all imaging devices, such as facsimile units, copiers, printers, and scanners. There will be a very long-term coexistence of paper documents and electronic documents.

CONCLUSION

The arrival of digital media brings a number of powerful new possibilities. Hayes (1993) raises an interesting point: "To society accustomed to writing on stone or clay, paper must have seemed terribly ephemeral stuff, vulnerable to fire and water, with inscribed marks that all too easily smudged or bleached away. And yet paper prevailed. Moses' tablets were stone, but the story of Moses was told on paper. The economic incentives were just too powerful to be ignored: With paper, information became far cheaper to record, to store and transport. Exactly the same considerations argue that a transition to paperless, electronic writing is now inevitable." Even though the "paperless" office envisioned with the dawn of the digital age is still some time away, the future impact of digital technologies on paper and print media cannot be ignored and some have already brought significant changes. Paper will not disappear, but its use will change structurally. The burgeoning of digital devices will affect the consumption of different grades of paper. Some grades will suffer (e.g., printed forms and envelopes) while others will be benefited. For example, the use of pre-printed forms has dropped severely as they are replaced by electronic versions (see Table 10.3). Over 70% of Global 2000 organizations are actively looking to put their paper forms online, according to Cardiff Software, Inc and the Gartner Group. Historically, the role of paper as a transferring medium has changed. Before the Industrial society, paper-based medium was the only effective medium of records and messages. In the Information society, the role of paper in the distribution of information is complementary and supportive (Rennel, 1984). Today, paper serves many functions such as transferring materialized symbols across space (e.g., as in the mail), but there is little reason to assume that information will continue to be primarily distributed by paper.

It is very hard to predict exactly what will happen to paper in the future, because there are a number of subtle interactions of forces and trends. For example, it seems that an entire generation that is growing up with new technology is likely to have different preferences toward the use of paper.

As indicated in previous chapters, the preference for reading printed text remains strong, despite different extents in preferences among different genders and cultures (e.g., American, Chinese, and Mexican). Paper is unlikely to disappear in the digital age, because reading print media is deeply embedded in tradition. Digital and print media have their unique advantages and limitations. Each plays a different role and serves the needs of users in different circumstances (see Table 6.7). Even though people will continue to read more from a screen than from a printed page, we must also keep in mind that readers' purposes and preferences are very diverse due to differences in gender and age, and that there is not a single format that is ideal to all. Paper will continue to survive in the digital age because there are too many reasons for its existence and a practical substitute has not been found. It is unlikely that digital media will render print media and physical libraries extinct in the foreseeable future.

REFERENCES

Adams, S. (1995). The Corporate Memory Concept. *The Electronic Library*, 13, 303–311.

American Forest & Paper Association. (2006). *2006 Statistics: Paper, Paperboard & Wood Pulp*. Washington, DC: American Forest & Paper Association.

Bolter, J.D. (1991). *Writing Spaces: The Computer, Hypertext, and the History of Writing*. Hillsdale, NJ: L. Erlbaum Associates, Publishers.

Bradley, M. (2005, December 12). What Ever Happened to the Paperless Office? *The Christian Science Monitor*. Retrieved August 25, 2007, from http://www.csmonitor.com/2005/1212/p13s01-wmgn.html.

Cuban, L. (1986). *Teachers and Machines: The Classroom Use of Technology since 1920*. New York, NY: Teachers College Press.

Griffiths, J. and King, D.W. (1993). *Special Libraries: Increasing the Information Edge*. Washington, DC: Special Library Association.

Hart, P.E. and Liu, Z. (2003). Trust in the Preservation of Digital Information. *Communications of the ACM*, 46(6), 93–97.

Hayes, B. (1993). The Information Age: The Electronic Palimpsest. *The Sciences*, 133(5), 10–13.

Hsu, R.C. and Mitchell, W.E. (1997). After 400 Years, Print Is Still Superior. *Communications of the ACM*, 40(10), 27–28.

Japan Paper Association (2007). *Outlook For Domestic Demand for Paper and Paperboard in 2007*. Retrieved August 25, 2007, from http://www.jpa.gr.jp/en/about/ann/domestic_text.pdf.

Kaufman, R. (1966). Data Systems that Cross Company Boundaries. *Harvard Business Review*, 44(1), 141–145.

Manguel, A. (1996). *A History of Reading*. New York, NY: Viking.

Marshall, C.C. (1997). Annotation: From Paper Books to the Digital Library. In *Proceedings of the 2nd ACM International Conference on Digital Libraries* (pp.131–140). New York, NY: ACM Press.

McKnight, C. (1997). Electronic Journals: What Do Users Think of Them? In *Proceedings of International Symposium on Research, Development and Practice in Digital Libraries*. Tsukuba, Japan. Retrieved June 23, 2008, from http://www.dl.slis.tsukuba.ac.jp/ISDL97/proceedings/mcknight.html.

The Office of the Future (1975, June 30). *Business Week*, 2387, 48–70. See also http://en.wikipedia.org/wiki/Paperless_office.

Olsen, J. (1994). *Electronic Journal Literature: Implications for Scholars*. London: Mecklermedia.

Rennel, J. (1984). *Future of Paper in the Telematic World*. Helsinki, Finland: A Jaakko Poyry Review.

Rivera, C. (2000). A Funny Thing Happen on the Way to the Paperless Office. *Office Solutions*, 17(10), 19.

Sciadas, G. (2006). *Our Lives in Digital Times*. Retrieved August 25, 2007, from http://www.statcan.ca/english/research/56F0004MIE/56F0004MIE2006014.pdf.

Sellen, A. and Harper, R. (2002). *The Myth of the Paperless Office*. Cambridge, MA: MIT Press.

Strassmann, P.A. (1985). *Information Payoff*. New York, NY: The Free Press.

Warnock, J. (1991). Electronic Paper: Fulfilling the Promise. *Publish*, 6, 120.

Williams, R. (1974). *Television*. New York, NY: Shochen Books.

INDEX

About the Author

DR. ZIMING LIU is an associate professor at San Jose State University. He received his Ph.D. in library and information studies at the University of California at Berkeley in 1996. He has published numerous papers in top-tier scholarly journals such as *Annual Review of Information Science and Technology*, *Communications of the ACM*, *Information Processing and Management*, *Journal of the American Society for Information Science and Technology*, and *Journal of Documentation*. Some of his publications have been translated and published internationally.